P HE
FAMILY?

PART OF THE FAMILY?

**Nannies,
Housekeepers,
Caregivers
and the Battle
for Domestic Workers' Rights**

SHEILA BAPAT

PUBLISHING

BROOKLYN, NEW YORK

Printed in the United States of America.
First Paperback Edition
10 9 8 7 6 5 4 3 2 1

Please direct inquiries to:
Ig Publishing, Inc
392 Clinton Avenue
Brooklyn, New York 11238
www.igpub.com

Library of Congress Cataloging-in-Publication Data

Bapat, Sheila, 1981-
  Part of the family? : nannies, housekeepers, caregivers and the battle for domestic workers' rights / Sheila Bapat.
    pages cm
    ISBN 978-1-935439-85-1 (paperback)
  1. Household employees. 2. Household employees--United States. 3. Household employees--Legal status, laws, etc. 4. Migrant labor--Legal status, laws, etc. 5. Household employees--Labor unions. 6. Emigration and immigration. I. Title.
  HD8039.D5.B37 2014
  331.7′61640973--dc23
                                    2014014553

For my mom, whose hard work made me who I am today.

CONTENTS

FOREWORD

A book that tells us the story of domestic workers is a victory in itself, because it gives overdue recognition to a forgotten sector of the labor force. It speaks against the marginalization of those workers and says, "Don't forget!" As American labor movements have won rights for other workers, domestic employees have historically been left behind. Their work is often devalued as menial. It is work that is unrecognized in the context of families and in the labor market. To win rights for domestic workers means to go up against the triple threat of class, race and gender barriers. To the modern equivalents of the upper crust we see in Downton Abbey, domestic work should be out of sight and out of mind. It is denigrated as the duty (not even real work) of women and is generally the employment realm of immigrants and women of color. We see the extreme form of this dehumanization in a celebrated case in which a diplomat in New York left the country, rather than face accusations that she underpaid and abused a nanny.

When I worked with the National Domestic Workers Alliance to write a Domestic Workers Bill of Rights for California, I knew I was going up against this kind of mindset. Too many people didn't understand why these workers should be brought under the umbrella of worker protections. I took inspiration from the New York version of the Domestic Worker Bill of Rights. We kept on with the valiant support of people like Sen. Kevin de León, whose mother rode the bus to clean houses when he was a boy, and institutions like the *New York Times*, which spoke up for these rights.

I knew how underpaid these women are. Many have wages that don't even work out to minimum wage. I was struck to hear that in many of their households, there is not enough money to keep food in the house all month long. They have to come to work sick and don't get time off to see a doctor. Nearly a quarter of them have been fired for calling in sick.

Despite the support, and despite the overwhelming need, our bill faced nasty attacks. It was mischaracterized as a "babysitter" bill. There were scare tactics aimed at disabled employers of care workers. There was an industry that wanted to maximize profits by keeping pay low. We worked for two years, only to have the bill vetoed at the last minute in 2012. It was a shock to me, and a terrible slap to the workers who advocated to bring the bill to the Governor's desk. I immediately committed to coming back with a new bill. The next time around, we prevailed and convinced the Governor to sign a bill for overtime pay, thanks in large part to high-profile women like Amy Poehler and Sandra Fluke, and of course thanks to the hundreds of domestic workers and their employers who worked tirelessly on AB 241. Ours was not the only victory in 2013. We also saw Hawaii enact a bill, and we saw moves at the federal level. New Department of Labor regulations that go into effect in 2015 will bring some relief to domestic workers across the country.

That isn't the end of the story, though. As this book shows, there is still work to be done around the United States, here in California, and throughout the world. But that's what worker struggles are like—you win the advances a step at a time. Sometimes, you work hard and face obstacles, as we did in 2012. Other states are still at that stage. Sometimes, you manage to make a big step forward. This book is a step forward.

—Tom Ammiano, Member of the California State Assembly

INTRODUCTION

"Care can never be valued if its givers are exploited."—
Michael Lyon, San Francisco Gray Panthers and Hand
in Hand

Chevy Chase, Maryland, is a charming, upper-crust town of just under one thousand residents. Maple and oak trees line the streets, and houses are worth nearly a million dollars. The median family income is about $140,000 per year. It was here that Fatima Cortessi, at the age of twenty, landed after leaving her home country of Paraguay in 2011.[1]

The deal that brought Fatima to America seemed—as it so often does for domestic workers—solid: $1,000 per month to clean, cook, and care for the children of a couple living in the United States. The first few months went smoothly, with Fatima settling into her new country. Though she spoke no English, the couple she was working for promised to help her enroll in English classes and possibly attend college.

Around month four of her new life in the United States, however, things began to fall apart for Fatima. First, the husband, also a native of Paraguay, became emotionally abusive. "You wouldn't be here if it wasn't for me. You owe me," he started telling her on a regular basis. In addition, the couple wouldn't always pay her regularly. When she asked for her money, Fatima would receive $100 or $150 at most. Not that Fatima had any time to spend her money, as her days began at six in the morning, when she fed the children and got them ready for school. After the kids left, Fatima would spend the rest of the morning cleaning the house and caring for the family dog. At two o'clock, the children would come home from school and Fatima would take care of them, cook for the family in the evening, and then clean up after everyone. If she was lucky, she'd be in bed by nine thirty or ten o'clock. She slept on a sofa in the basement, which she shared with the dog. And she worked weekends as well.

At some point, the couple Fatima was working for separated and moved into different homes. Fatima's job became twice as hard, as she was now responsible for cleaning both houses, for the same amount of money. Since she had never been taught how to use the local public transit system, she was required to ride a bike from one house to the other—while taking the dog with her.

This situation continued for a year and a half, at which point the couple said they could no longer afford to pay Fatima the same amount of money; she was forced to find work cleaning other homes while still working for her original family part-time. Eventually, she shared her story with one of her new employers. "They can't do this to you," the woman said, after Fatima revealed the saga of the past eighteen months of her life. The woman told Fatima about Casa de Maryland, an immigrant rights organization. It was there that Fatima met attorney Sheena Wadhawan. And that was when Fatima's life began to change.

Advocates from Casa de Maryland helped Fatima move out of the home she had been living in for the past eighteen months. Wadhawan determined that the couple owed Fatima upward of $30,000, and Fatima sued for unpaid wages and overtime. Of critical importance to Fatima's case, Maryland law does not exclude domestic workers from overtime pay—as a number of states do. The couple offered to settle for $10,000, and Fatima ultimately accepted their offer. Tired of letting this couple control her life, Fatima just wanted to move on. She now lives a life free of abuse, earns money cleaning houses, and is learning English through classes organized by Casa de Maryland. She also attends weekly meetings with other women who have experienced this type of employment abuse. "I had such low self-esteem because of this situation," Fatima says. "And Casa de Maryland helped me regain my self-confidence."

Casa de Maryland has been working on immigrant rights issues since its founding in 1985 by Central American refugees. In response to a growing need among immigrant populations, the organization now focuses extensively on low-income workers, with a special concentration on women.[2] Casa de Maryland is among the many multiethnic community organizing and legal aid nonprofits throughout the country that have built the foundation of today's domestic workers' movement—acting as "domestic insurgents," as one article dubbed them.[3]

Not all domestic workers' experiences are rife with mistreatment, as Fatima Cortessi's was. Like most sectors, domestic work encompasses a range of situations and environments. Fatima's experience was far different, for example, from that of Tania, a nineteen-year-old nanny in Oakland, California. "For Tania, we are like her extended family," says Meg Yardley, Tania's employer and a member of Hand in Hand, a national network of employers of nannies, house cleaners and home attendants. Tania cares for Meg's two children, her four-year-old daughter, Laurel, and her four-month-old son, Owen.[4] "Tania would come over for work and Laurel would be so happy to see Tania that her whole body would wiggle," Meg says. "I need to work to earn enough for my family, and I really like my job. So it feels good to leave my children with someone they love." Tania is now expecting her first baby. When the child comes, she will care for Meg's children along with her own.

Fatima and Tania's contrasting stories reflect the uncertainty and luck inherent in domestic labor. Whether a domestic worker will be treated with fairness and dignity or exploited and abused depends on the whims, character, and awareness of her employer as well as where in the world she happens to be. And what exacerbates this uncertainty encourages this subjectivity is the variable legal status of the work itself: domestic workers are far less likely to be protected by the laws that regulate most other sectors of employment. Globally, more than 40 percent of domestic workers are not legally entitled to earn a minimum wage, while one-third are not eligible for maternity leave.[5] And this is despite the fact that domestic work is a swiftly expanding sector of the global economy, having grown from thirty-two million domestic workers worldwide in 1999 to eighty to one hundred million today, fifteen million of whom are children.[6] Nearly 85 percent of domestic workers today are women. According to the International Labour Organization (ILO), approximately one in thirteen wage-earning women in the world are domestic laborers.[7]

In the United States alone, numerous key labor and employment regulations, including the Fair Labor Standards Act (FLSA), the National Labor Relations Act (NLRA), and various occupational safety regulations, have historically excluded domestic workers. The nearly two million domestic workers in the United States—and the millions worldwide—are treated as a casual, ancillary part of the workforce, neglected by labor laws, even as they take on the most crucial work for families and communities, cleaning homes and caring for children and the elderly.[8] Even when there are protections in place, many domestic workers like Fatima are from foreign countries, do not speak the local language well, face challenges negotiating wages and terms of employment, and are often unaware of their rights. Love and compassion are a central part of being a nanny or caregiver, yet many live and labor in subpar conditions and receive little or no respect for their work, in addition to being excluded from legal protections.

A movement to establish labor protections for domestic workers, and to render them visible in political and economic terms, has gained impressive momentum worldwide over the last fifteen years. Multiple actors in the feminist-labor-activist realms—including nonprofit advocacy and legal organizations like Casa de Maryland, traditional labor unions, lawyers, and policymakers representing many diverse ethnic groups—have deepened their advocacy on behalf of domestic workers, appealing directly to the public to build support. These efforts have resulted in concrete policy and cultural changes, bringing to light the value of domestic work and the systemic exclusion of domestic workers from labor protections. The first major victory of the movement was the passage of New York State's Domestic Workers' Bill of Rights in 2010, which affected an estimated two hundred thousand domestic workers. California and Hawaii have since followed suit.[9]

Activism in the United States is fostering change at the international level as well, evidenced by the ILO passing the Domestic Workers Convention, along with increased activism among domestic workers in multiple countries, including Brazil, India, and Singapore.[10] Activism abroad is perhaps even more crucial, given that the situation of domestic workers in non-Western countries is often far more dire than that of domestic workers in the United States.[11] Despite some significant setbacks along the way—including Governor Jerry Brown's veto of California's Domestic Workers' Bill of Rights in 2012—the movement for domestic workers' rights has quickly achieved policy reforms and has the potential to transform over the long term the ways in which domestic labor is valued throughout the world.

Above all else, the movement is cultivating the leadership of domestic workers themselves, who have been central to the lobbying and legislative activities being undertaken on their behalf. "Know-your-rights" trainings and community organizing are becoming common practices among domestic workers in many cities in the United States, as well as globally. The movement is also an illustration of how labor law has evolved, with change no longer driven by behemoth legislation like the NLRA but by smaller-scale, group-based advocacy. The movement's objective does not end with more regulations; the overarching goal is achieving empowerment and justice for a vulnerable population of workers, revealing domestic labor's value to the broader economy, and establishing its social and cultural dignity.

This book focuses on the ways in which the current movement empowers domestic workers in the United States and globally to advocate for themselves. Beginning with an analysis of domestic labor's roots in slavery, this book explores the specific ways in which preeminent labor laws have failed to recognize domestic labor historically, as well as early attempts by domestic workers to address these failures. Subsequent chapters focus on the emergence of the current domestic workers' movement, in particular its strategies and leadership. Finally, this book analyzes the domestic workers' movement in the broader context of modern labor trends and considers the implications of immigration reform and the waning influence of traditional unions. Fundamentally, this is a book about activism; about the vision and leadership of that activism, the ways that activism is influencing policy in the United States, and the impact of US-based activism on workers in the rest of the world.

What Is Domestic Work, and Why Isn't It Valued?

A key premise of this book is that domestic labor is generally believed to be void of economic value, and that the current movement for domestic workers' rights is doing critical work to change this perception. But before delving more deeply into this idea, it is worth discussing what "domestic work" is, why it should be included within labor protections, and how it contributes to the economy.

The National Domestic Workers Alliance issued a report in 2012 presenting survey data about the treatment of domestic workers nationally. The report's foreword, written by author and activist Barbara Ehrenreich, describes exactly what domestic work is and why it is unique:

> Domestic work is, by necessity, intensely personal in nature. A nanny is entrusted with the care and well-being of the employers' most precious loved ones. She is a witness to all the family's foibles and dysfunctions, sometimes even a confidante to her employers. Though a housecleaner may make little verbal contact with her employers, they have few secrets from her. She changes their sheets, dusts their desktops, scrubs their bathroom counters, and sometimes overhears their quarrels. The caretaker for an elderly or disabled person often functions explicitly as a companion, providing conversation and emotional support, as well as help with dressing and bathing.[12]

The report goes on to point out the differences between "reproductive"—work performed within the domestic or private sphere—and "productive" economies, and how each one is valued, or devalued:

> Domestic work is unseen in the way that most work dedicated to cleaning and caring is unseen. At the end of

the domestic worker's day, no durable goods or consumer products have been created or distributed; neither the flow of capital nor the accumulation of profits has been directly served. Instead, a child is another day older and still safe and healthy. An elderly parent is well fed and attended to. The absence of dirt on a kitchen floor is silent witness to a laboring hand. In a capital-dominant world, work that does not appear to produce value or facilitate its exchange is devalued and rendered socially invisible. Yet this labor, whether performed by a family member or by an employee, supports and subsidizes all other productive work.[13]

Consistent with the invisible nature of "women's work," the legal history of domestic work has been one of exclusion from protection and recognition. What is at the root of this sweeping, global, systemic failure of law and policy to protect people who take on the caring responsibilities for homes, children, and elders? What causes ordinarily "upstanding" people of means to mistreat other human beings so egregiously? Unfortunately, contemporary feminist dialogue has failed to provide us with a better understanding of these questions. Until relatively recently, not many feminist thinkers and writers focused on this issue. In a 2013 article in *Dissent* titled "Trickle-Down Feminism," author Sarah Jaffe wrote about how feminist energy has been misplaced, with writers devoting countless articles to dissecting the every move of wealthy superwomen like Yahoo CEO Marissa Mayer instead of the economic trends that impact so many more women's lives, such as the rapid growth of domestic work.[14]

Despite this gap in modern-day feminist writing, decades of feminist theory have addressed this question of how to value reproductive labor through an examination of the economics of the public and private spheres, and our socio-cultural perceptions of each. The intimacy inherent to domestic work is sometimes given as the argument for why domestic work should not be included within labor protections: it is supposed to be work that comes from the heart, rooted in love, an extension of a woman's "natural" tendencies—thus not necessarily worthy of compensation or labor protections.[15] However, the fallacy of this framework has been clear to feminists for years. Writers from Gloria Steinem to Angela Harris to Mariarosa Dalla Costa have shed light on the view that domestic labor is labor worthy of economic value. A confluence of contemporary circumstances is finally enabling theories and understandings of the domestic sphere to take shape as policy and cultural change.

Historically, feminist theory helped establish the framework within which domestic labor is now being recognized in law and policy, and which guides the consciousness of many domestic workers' rights advocates today. Take Mariarosa Dalla Costa and Selma James's *The Power of Women and the Subversion of Community*, a pamphlet published in 1972.[16] By using a "feminist reading of Marx to challenge the left orthodoxy on the role of women," Dalla Costa and James were among the first to apply Marxism to the gendered division of labor, analyzing how domestic labor has always been completely invisible to capital markets:

> Serving men and children in wageless isolation had hidden that we were serving capital. Now we know that we are not only indispensable to capitalist production in those countries where we are 45% of their waged labour force. We are always their indispensable workforce, at home, cleaning, washing and ironing; making, disciplining and bringing up babies; servicing men physically, sexually and emotionally[17]

Dalla Costa and James also praised the ideas of Malcolm X and other black intellectuals who tied together the relationship between racial injustice and labor inequality; they applied all these principles to their organizing work, reflected in the International Wages for Housework Campaign, founded by James, which demanded that the government compensate work that took place inside the home. Dalla Costa and James's relevance is clear today, with the domestic workers' movement slowly shifting legal, societal, and cultural opinions about what type of labor ought to be valued, who performs the labor that is valued, and why some labor is generally invisible to capital markets. Barbara Ehrenreich remarked upon their work in 2000, stating that "Marxist feminists Mariarosa Dalla Costa and Selma James proposed in 1972 that the home was in fact an economically productive and significant workplace, an extension of the actual factory, since housework served to 'reproduce the labor power' of others, particularly men."[18]

In her 1994 essay "Revaluing Economics," Gloria Steinem argued that labor is valued in accordance with prevailing social constructs about race, sex, and class. Jobs in high finance are valued with comfortable compensation, for example, while the work of caring for people is often deemed unworthy of a minimum wage. "Categories of work are less likely to be paid by the expertise they require—or even by importance to the community or to the often mythical free market—than by the sex, race and class of most of their workers," Steinem wrote.[19] The sex, race, and class of domestic workers are overwhelmingly female, non-white, and low-income or poor.

Consistent with Steinem's analysis, America's relationship to those who work within the domestic sphere has long been troubled and generally starved of the political will to protect and regulate. Slavery, which was legal in the United States until 1865 and still exists globally to varying degrees, has influenced how domestic laborers are currently treated. In addition to having no legal freedom or power over their own lives, slaves who labored in American homes were subject to unspeakable cruelty, sexual assault, and abuse. As the United States has evolved away from slavery to New Deal–era labor policies and to an economy influenced by globalization, the line connecting slavery to paid domestic work continues to be deeply intertwined. The blog Gender Across Borders corroborates this idea, noting, "In patriarchal power dynamics, domestic work is typically assigned to a woman of the household. In a society with great income disparities, if this woman is rich, she can delegate her domestic work to another, poorer woman."[20]

Scholar V. Spike Peterson discusses the economic value of "subject formation," which is what rearing children and caring for adults is all about:

Feminists have long argued that subject formation matters structurally for economic relations. It produces individuals who are then able to "work" and this unpaid reproductive labour saves capital the costs of producing key inputs. It also instills attitudes, identities and belief systems that enable societies to function.[21]

Peterson goes on to discuss the irony of how pro-family ideology and the romanticization of childbirth and rearing does not equate to economic support for these activities:

In spite of romanticised motherhood and a glut of profamily rhetoric, neoliberal globalisation reduces the emotional, cultural and material resources necessary for the wellbeing of most women and families.... Women everywhere are increasing the time they spend on reproductive labour, in ensuring food availability and health maintenance for the family, in providing emotional support and taking responsibility for young, ill and elderly dependents. Mothers often curtail their own consumption and healthcare in favour of serving family needs, and daughters (more often than sons) forfeit educational opportunities when extra labour is needed at home.[22]

Peterson points out that this enhanced stress and pressure to serve the domestic sphere, and the lack of resources in support of that service, impacts whole families and communities:

The effects are not limited to women because the increased burdens they bear are inevitably translated into costs to their families, and hence to societies more generally.

Peterson also explains domestic work in the context of the "informal economy" and its impact on the "formal" or "productive" economy:

Domestic labor, or social reproduction, produces labor power (workers) upon which the formal economy depends. One important effect is that this "free" (unpaid) labor benefits employers, who do not have to pay the full costs of producing the labor force.

Feminist scholars have also pointed out the exclusion of domestic workers from New Deal–era labor rights legislation under the FLSA, the NLRA, the Social Security Act, or the

Occupational Safety and Health Administration (OSHA). As Angela Harris has noted:

> The creation of the idea of two spheres, private and public, is integral to a structural liberalism framework that continues to redistribute wealth and power upwards. The creation of a private sphere that should be free from government intervention is at the heart of the continued subjugation of domestic workers. It is a distinction invented by White supremacy and heteropatriarchy, and codified into law in key locations that facilitate the exploitation of Black and immigrant women.[23]

Labor patterns that emerged during the Industrial Revolution illustrate Peterson's and Harris's assertions. Attorney and scholar Terri Nilliasca also points out that

> domestic work is women's work. The Industrial Revolution led to a restructuring of the family that required a new, gendered division of work. Work dealing with the reproduction of labor such as child care, food preparation, household maintenance, and elder care was relegated to the "private" unpaid sphere.... The "cult of domesticity" arose in the first half of the nineteenth century, solidifying boundaries between the "public" and the "private" home sphere. The heterosexual family became sanctified as a respite from the competitive industrial world, and women became responsible for the creation of that sanctuary. The resulting regulatory and legal frameworks furthered this social construction, treating "housework as indistinguishable from other private family matters while treating paid labor as relevant to legal doctrine."[24]

The consequence of this exclusion is that private-sphere laborers exist in an underworld unattached by the regulations, codes, and mores that govern public-sphere work. Legal scholar Janie A. Chuang wrote in a 2010 essay that "labeling housework as 'care' signals that work in the home is divorced from economic entitlements. Labor rights considered normal in the formal economy (e.g., minimum wage, days off, vacation, and fixed working hours) are not viewed as necessary or even appropriate in the context of work in a private household."[25]

The Current Political Surge

With feminist theory serving as a philosophical foundation, the social movement for greater awareness about domestic workers' rights is growing, building alliances with feminist and political leaders of a variety of stripes, and effectively utilizing social media. It is clear that setbacks—such as Governor Brown's 2012 veto in California—do not deter the tenacious organizers at the National Domestic Workers Alliance, Caring Across Generations, Jobs with Justice, and other groups that are mobilizing domestic workers around the country, advocating for state and federal policy changes, and raising awareness among employers and high-profile leaders within a wide range of movements.

This book will explore the roots of this rising movement, its strategies and successes, as well as why, after such a long history of exclusion, the conditions are ripe for expanded protections and standards for domestic workers. Against the backdrop of the current economy—rife with unemployment, part-time employment, and contract and freelance work, and with fewer and fewer opportunities for security or chances to climb out of poverty—many of the themes that these advocates are fighting for bleed into the experiences of American workers generally.

Sick days, paid vacation, and paid family leave continue to be rarities for many workers. The domestic workers' rights movement is helping to elevate American consciousness about how the individual worker ought to be treated—and how our policies can evolve to match this aspiration. The movement is multiethnic, reflective of not only the changing immigrant and racial demographics of America but specifically the impact of feminist ideology on women of color and how race, gender, and ideology are intersecting.

Why, after centuries of exclusion, is this surge of activism occurring at this point in time (rather than, for example, during the New Deal era, when workers in America were first claiming their rights)? Priscilla Gonzalez, who for ten years was the leader of Domestic Workers United, believes the reason is "intersectional feminist thought coupled with the increase of women of color and immigrant women in the US feminist community."[26] Intersectional feminist analysis has evolved in the United States to the point where feminist women of color, often the children of immigrants, are putting forward a vision for justice that is winning funding, political and cultural allies, and major legislative reforms that for the first time recognize and include domestic work. As this book will note, though domestic workers have organized before, the recent surge of sustained and successful activism is unprecedented. "This iteration of organizing domestic workers has been most sustained, and I feel like in general, a lot of organizing efforts were hard to sustain in prior time periods," says Gonzalez, adding, "And this is in part because our vision is not limited to just wanting to win rights for domestic workers." According to Gonzalez, movement leaders like Ai-jen Poo, director of the National Domestic Workers Alliance, are third-wave feminists who understand intersectional analysis and how domestic workers are not just women, are not just workers, are not just immigrants, are not just women of color, but are all of these things. "Ai-jen and the other leaders of this movement understand that we needed to move on many different fronts: in the labor spaces, in the women's rights spaces," Gonzalez says. "We have never believed in silos. We have always made these natural bridges. We do not compartmentalize identities. There is a key shift among feminists of color in this country. That is one important piece that is generating the current domestic workers' movement."

Intersectional feminist thinking and practice is the most important influence in this movement for dignity and basic standards for workers who care for people young, ill, and old. In addition to grasping the importance of asserting their personal identities, domestic workers know the importance of love and compassion in their work—and they are now joining with their fellow domestic workers to harness this love and compassion to improve their lives.

1. Slavery and Domestic Work—Then and Now

"Pity me, and pardon me, O virtuous reader! You never knew what it is to be a slave; to be entirely unprotected by law or custom; to have the laws reduce you *to the condition of a chattel, entirely subject to the will of another.* You never exhausted your ingenuity in avoiding the snares, and eluding the power of a hated tyrant; you never shuddered at the sound of his footsteps, and trembled within hearing of his voice."—**Harriet Jacobs**, writer and house slave, Edenton, North Carolina (emphasis added)[1]

In 2013, writer-director Quentin Tarantino won an Academy Award for his screenplay for the film *Django Unchained*. Set in the late 1850s, the movie tells the story of Django, a vigilante slave played by Jamie Foxx, who is given his freedom and then proceeds to kill several slave owners in order to rescue his wife, Broomhilda, a "house slave" for an evil plantation owner. The film explicitly portrays the physical and sexual abuse Broomhilda is forced to endure as she labors inside the white man's home.

Consistent with the androcentric nature of many of his films, Tarantino's primary focus in *Django* is not on the house slaves, who, historically, were typically female.[2] Rather, the women in Tarantino's story merely support the goals of the macho Django. Artist and writer Remeike Forbes points out that

> not only are women marginal in the movie, but the central female character, Django's wife Broomhilda, is afforded only a few lines. Her key role [is] as the damsel-

in-distress, [whom] the hero must rescue from a "circle of fire"..... Unfortunately, Broomhilda is also the most rebellious female character. The other black women who appear in the film are just the usual fare of fawning house slaves—"as you please, Big Daddy"—or pleasured concubines.[3]

Even though—or perhaps because—the film is steeped in this gender problem, the treatment of house slaves in 1850s America, as depicted in *Django Unchained*, is relevant to the treatment of current-day domestic workers. In many ways, the experiences of nineteenth-century house slaves foretold the story of today's domestic workers, and there remains a connection between pre-emancipation slavery and modern-day human trafficking. The difference is that trafficking victims and other domestic workers are better able to seek justice from abuse or mistreatment at the hands of their employers—because of the domestic workers' movement.

Domestic Slavery

While some historical accounts indicate that house slaves received less egregious treatment than those who worked in the fields, according to Harriet Jacobs, a nineteenth century writer and house slave from North Carolina, living inside the slave owner's home was pure hell.[4] Jacobs writes how on Sundays her mistress "would station herself in the kitchen, and wait till [dinner] was dished, and then spit in all the kettles and pans...to prevent the cook and her children from eking out their meager fare with the remains of the gravy and other scrapings." Jacobs goes on to detail how "provisions were weighed out by the pound and ounce, three times a day," and that her mistress "knew how many biscuits a quart of flour would make, and exactly what size they ought to be."

Whether a house slave was mistreated or not depended on the whims of the slave owner. And, as with many of today's immigrant domestic workers, there was no way for a slave to control whether she worked for a gentle master or an abusive one. This uncertainty put house slaves in uniquely vulnerable situations, given the intimacy they shared with the families for whom they worked. Even as they were susceptible to physical, sexual, and emotional abuse, house slaves were also responsible for caring for families and running households, serving as personal servants to their masters and mistresses, and producing the food used by everyone on the plantation. They were commonly on call twenty-four hours a day.

Living in the master's house also meant that house slaves lacked the support and camaraderie of other slaves, which at times made them more susceptible to physical and sexual assault. A physically attractive female house slave could be particularly vulnerable. Harriet Jacobs wrote, "If God has bestowed beauty upon a slave woman, it will prove her greatest curse. That which commands admiration in the white woman only hastens the degradation of the female slave."[5] In addition, many women slaves—house slaves or not—were forced to bear the children of their masters.[6]

Other conditions in which nineteenth-century house slaves toiled persist for domestic workers today, particularly those who live with their employers. For example, many household workers are expected to be available 24/7, are supervised closely by their employers as Harriet Jacobs was, and are vulnerable to their employers' moods. Barbara Ehrenreich describes this intimacy of working inside the home as the key distinction between labor in the domestic and public spheres:

Someone who stocks shelves in a big box store is unlikely to even know the names of anyone higher up in the corporate hierarchy than the store manager, who in turn may know his or her frontline employees only as a "labor cost." In contrast...most domestic workers are employed directly by the families they serve. They work in their employers' homes. They may even live in their employers' homes, perhaps sleeping in one of the children's rooms.[7]

In addition to themes of exploitation and abuse, the perception of domestic labor as ancillary or irrelevant to the "productive" economy has also been a feature of care work since America's earliest days. Early codes regulating indentured servitude in the United States reveal that both slave and non-slave domestic labor were legally deemed to have no economic value. The Virginia House of Burgesses was one of the first elected bodies in the United States to grapple with how the law would codify slavery and indentured servitude based on whether the work took place inside or outside the home.[8] In 1643, farmers and business owners were subject to a tithing, or tax, for their black female and male, as well as white male, servants who worked in the fields, and who were therefore seen as producing wealth. By contrast, white women servants did not trigger a tax, because "the law presumed they worked inside the home and were not producing wealth."[9] Domestic work was also viewed, in both the slavery and post-slavery eras, as "nigger's work" and "women's work," a combination that contributed to and exacerbated its lack of economic value. Legal scholars Marci Seville and Hina Shah have written about how "the mammy image—a large, maternal figure with a headscarf and almost always a wide-toothed grin—persists as the most enduring racial caricature of African-American women. The racial disdain for the black servant—'a despised race to a despised calling'—justified labeling the work as 'nigger's work.'"[10] Adding another layer to that disdain, domestic work was also considered to be "women's work" and thus a "'labor of love'…'outside the boundary of the world's economy.'"[11]

Slavery also reinforced existing racial hierarchies between white and black women. Terri Nilliasca, a legal scholar who also works for the labor union Unite Here, unpacks the particular relationship of black women's labor to that of white women in the pre-emancipation era:

> During slavery, the labor of Black women facilitated the ability of White women to live up to an idealized standard of femininity, one in which a White woman was able to fulfill the gendered division of work without actually getting her hands dirty. In the Southeast United States, it was the enslaved African woman's labor that enabled the aristocratic White woman's lifestyle. Thus, true womanhood was defined as "virtuous, pure, and white," and proper Black womanhood was defined as service to the creation of that White woman ideal. Domestic service was part of the racial caste system, such that no "self-respecting, native- born Southern white woman" would take such a job. Many White women accepted and perpetuated this racist division of labor in order to elevate their status in heteropatriarchy. The creation of the racist stereotype of Mammy is the quintessential embodiment of the ideal of the Black woman in service to the White woman. Mammy gladly raised White children as her own and in sacrifice of her biological Black children.[12]

In its report, "Home Economics," the National Domestic Workers Alliance pointed out the racial aspect of domestic labor, namely that female slaves were among the earliest domestic laborers in the United States. Unfortunately, that most domestic work is performed by women who lack full agency over their own lives and bodies is a reality that has not disappeared.

Modern-Day Slavery: Trafficking and Domestic Laborers

In 2006, seventeen-year-old Shanti Gurung moved from her home in India to New York City with her new employer, Neena Malhotra. Shanti left behind her family, friends, and everything she knew for what promised to be a secure job and an exciting opportunity: to live with and work for a privileged Indian family in the United States. Malhotra was an Indian diplomat who lived with her husband in a Manhattan apartment. The couple offered Shanti a verbal employment contract promising her room and board and at least $108 per month in wages, in exchange for "light cooking, light cleaning, and staffing the occasional house party."[13]

Much like the experience of Fatima Cortessi, Shanti Gurung's reality turned out to be far different than she originally envisioned. For the three years she worked in the Malhotra household, Shanti was regularly denied food, forced to sleep on the floor even though the Malhotras' large apartment included several unoccupied bedrooms, and made to work more than sixteen hours per day. During those three years, Shanti's weight dropped from 147 pounds to a fragile 84 pounds. The Malhotras also hid Shanti's passport and visa, prohibited her from calling her family in India, and told her repeatedly that if she ran away, Homeland Security would rape her, torture her, and "ship her back to India like cargo."[14]

Eventually, using her small savings, Shanti fled the Malhotras' apartment in 2010, seeking help from a woman she had recently met in a grocery store. After escaping her abusive employers, Shanti discovered Adhikaar, a New York City organization that works with the local Nepali community. The group connected

Shanti to critical resources—specifically, to Amy Tai, an attorney with the Urban Justice Center's Community Development Project. After sharing Shanti's situation, Tai, who works with a network of private law firms' pro bono practices, was able to secure a lawyer from the international law firm Gibson, Dunn and Crutcher to represent Shanti in a suit against the Malhotras.[15] It is not standard practice for big law firms to insert themselves in matters involving domestic workers' rights unless there is substantial abuse and potential for a settlement; that the firm took the case demonstrates just how egregious Shanti's situation was. On March 16, 2012, the Southern District of New York ordered that Shanti Gurung be awarded nearly $1.5 million in damages. The Court found that under the Fair Labor Standards Act (FLSA), Shanti was entitled to back wages in accordance with New York's minimum wage—a higher wage than the federal minimum wage. Shanti was also awarded breach of contract damages, federal and state liquidated damages, and damages for emotional distress. Notably, Shanti's judgment also included overtime relief, as prescribed by New York State's Domestic Workers' Bill of Rights. Prior to the 2010 passage of the bill, FLSA exempted live-in workers from the overtime requirement.

Unfortunately, the case of Shanti Gurung is all too representative of the harsh treatment of many domestic workers at the hands of foreign diplomats. In 2008, the Government Accountability Office (GAO) issued a report identifying at least forty-two cases of abuse of domestic servants by foreign diplomats since the year 2000. The report concluded that the US government's efforts to reduce the incidence of abuse by foreign diplomats against domestic workers could be improved.[16] It also stated that the number of cases of abuse could potentially be much greater, because many abused household workers are afraid of reaching out to authorities. The report also found that diplomatic immunity, secured in the 1960s by the Vienna Convention on Diplomatic Relations, is an effective shield for diplomats from criminal prosecution and civil suits, and presents a major barrier to justice for domestic workers.[17]

The problem is particularly acute in New York City and Washington, DC, where foreign diplomats typically reside. Ivy Suriyopas, director of the Anti-Trafficking Initiative with the Asian American Legal Defense and Education Fund, has been an anti-trafficking advocate in New York City for nearly a decade. According to Suriyopas, New York and Washington, DC, are "hotbeds for diplomatic and consular activity. We have identified a number of domestic workers trafficked into consular households. Manhattan is a stratified city but there is lots of wealth too; there are a number of families in need of domestic workers but who do not want to pay or follow basic standards."[18]

The US State Department currently issues A-3 visas for workers of diplomatic personnel and their families, and G-5 visas for workers of foreign officials for international organizations including the World Bank and the United Nations. Janie A. Chuang of the American University Washington College of Law points out that visas are not tied to the worker but rather to the diplomat, providing the domestic worker with lawful status only during the working arrangement.[19] When applying for the visa, diplomats must produce an employment contract stating that they will follow US labor laws, offer information about scope of work and payment schedules, as well as agreeing not take away the worker's passport or visa, or require the worker to remain at work after hours without compensation. However, these provisions are not necessarily adhered to, as the case of Shanti Gurung illustrates. The State Department's Foreign Affairs Manual sets forth what the working conditions for employees of diplomats ought to be, but these are not enforceable.[20] In addition, exploited workers rarely receive copies of their employment contracts, and the US consular offices only recently began keeping copies of the contracts themselves.[21] Even if protections were stronger, exploited workers are often too fearful of retaliation against their families in their home countries, or afraid for their own physical safety, to risk speaking up.

As Shanti Gurung's story demonstrates, the adoption of the Thirteenth Amendment in 1865 outlawing slavery did not end demand for or supply of free or cheap domestic labor in the United States. On the contrary, US policy has long enabled the importation of cheap domestic laborers but excluded these workers from legal protections. For example, Congress passed the Alien Contract Labor Act in 1885, "to prohibit the importation and migration of foreigners and aliens under contract or agreement to perform labor in the United States, its territories, and the District of Columbia."[22] The purpose of the act was to prevent cheap, unskilled labor from penetrating American borders and lowering wages. Yet the importation of domestic workers by other foreigners, such as diplomats, was explicitly permitted under the act.[23]

Even as the right of workers to labor protections took root as an American value during the New Deal, US policy continued to allow some employers to pay little or no wages to workers who had difficulty advocating for their rights. Says Nelson Lichtenstein of the Center for the Study of Work, Labor, and Democracy at the University of California, Santa Barbara, "Employers for a century have been trying to import workers who have something less than full citizenship." He adds that from a management perspective, "They're the perfect workers."[24]

The role of capitalism in this mix is clear. Tayyab Mahmud, director of the Center for Global Justice at the Seattle University School of Law, has written that "the construct of free wage-labor, envisaged as consensual sale of labor-power by an autonomous and unencumbered individual in a market of juridical equals governed strictly by economic laws of supply and demand, is the bedrock of the purportedly universal category of labor under capitalism."[25] The vestiges of slavery flourish along with this demand, as does the economic vulnerability of people who provide cheap labor.

As far in the past as slavery may seem, the practice continues to play a role in today's America. Domestic servitude in the United States (and around the world) influences how many domestic workers are treated, and is often rife with abuse. Legally termed "human trafficking," the abuse of domestic workers includes the denial of compensation, the demand that laborers work around the clock, and, above all else, the threat or infliction of physical or emotional abuse. The International Labour Organization (ILO) estimates that 2.4 million people are trafficked worldwide each year, about 17,500 of them in the United States.[26] Over the years, human trafficking specifically for labor purposes has continued to plague the United States: in 2012, a report released by California attorney general Kamala Harris pointed out that many of those who are trafficked into or within the United States each year are hired into domestic labor situations.[27] According to the US government's *Trafficking in Persons Report*:

> A century and a half [after emancipation], slavery persists in the United States and around the globe, and many victims' stories remain sadly similar to those of the past. It is estimated that as many as 27 million men, women, and children around the world are victims of what is now often described with the umbrella term "human trafficking." The work that remains in combating this crime is the work of fulfilling the promise of freedom—freedom

from slavery for those exploited and the freedom for survivors to carry on with their lives.[28]

While human trafficking is often associated primarily with sex trafficking, labor trafficking is in fact more common, but far less likely to be reported.[29] Commercial sexual exploitation represents a sizeable part of forced labor and tends to be more widely known and understood among the general public, but the majority of forced laborers actually engage in domestic, agricultural, or sweatshop labor; work in nail salons, factories, construction projects, farming, or hotels.[30] There are approximately 8.1 million forced laborers in the non-sex economy around the world, and it is estimated that the United States profits to the tune of $4.5 billion annually through labor trafficking, equaling approximately $4,500 per laborer.[31] Worldwide, $32 billion is made annually by the exploitation of trafficked victims.

Trafficking victims who end up in domestic servitude are often imprisoned or forced to live in the homes of their employers, who confiscate their passports and other documents. From 2007 through 2012, the United States human trafficking hotline received nearly nine hundred calls related to domestic servitude.[32] And given how daunting it is for most trafficked victims to ask for help, many illegal or exploitative situations are believed to go unreported. Much like Shanti Gurung, who lived through unbearable conditions for over three years, many trafficked victims either never seek help or wait until their lives are hanging by a thread.

The Shield of Diplomatic Immunity

Compounding the lack of protections for domestic workers who work for diplomats, the diplomats themselves are immune from prosecution for the crimes they commit against their workers.

Under the Vienna Convention on Diplomatic Relations, a current diplomatic agent enjoys near absolute immunity from civil jurisdiction. This immunity is given full effect under United States law, pursuant to the Diplomatic Relations Act, which states that "any action or proceeding brought against an individual who is entitled to immunity with respect to such action or proceeding under the [VCDR] ... shall be dismissed."[33] As the preamble to the VCDR recognizes, "The purpose of such ... immunit[y] is not to benefit individuals but to ensure the efficient performance of functions of diplomatic missions as representing States."[34]

Under the Vienna Convention, diplomats can argue that their position as a state officeholder means they cannot be held liable for crimes they commit against people who work in their homes. However, there are narrow exceptions to diplomatic immunity, including:

1. A real action relating to private immovable property.
2. An action relating to succession.
3. An action relating to any professional or commercial activity exercised by the diplomatic agent in the receiving State outside his official functions.[35]

There is a dispute as to whether "domestic labor" is considered a commercial activity. As the American Bar Association points out in its guide *Meeting the Legal Needs of Human Trafficking Victims*:

> Many advocates contend that hiring a domestic servant also constitutes a commercial activity. Circuits are split on this issue. A suit brought under the Vienna Convention disagreed with that view, although a suit brought under the Foreign Sovereign Immunities Act, *did* recognize domestic work as a commercial activity.... The

arguments for the commercial activities exception to apply are arguably weaker in the context of an intersections case where there is not likely to be any formal hiring process or contractual employment relationship[36]

In actuality, however, the commercial activities exception has not often been a successful way of securing relief for domestic workers, given how expansive the reach of diplomatic immunity tends to be.[37] The only times domestic workers have been able to obtain legal judgments against their diplomat employers have been *after* the employers' service ended and they no longer held diplomatic status, a far more narrow status known as "residual immunity."[38]

In 2009, Vishranthamma Swarna became the first domestic servant to win a default judgment against her diplomat employer based on the theory of residual immunity. Since a former diplomat has immunity only for "'acts performed . . . in the exercise of his functions as a member of the mission,'" the court had to determine whether Vishranthamma's employer's actions were "private acts," and therefore not covered by immunity, or "official acts," which fell within residual immunity. The court ruled that the diplomat's hiring of Swarna was not connected with his diplomatic role with the state because, as attorney Jennifer Hoover Kappus has written, "the employment of a household worker was intended strictly to manage his personal affairs, and thus did not fall within Article 3 of the Vienna Convention which stipulates the official functions of a diplomat."[39] While the ruling in this case is encouraging, deeper reforms of the Vienna Convention are necessary to ensure that workers are able to hold their diplomat employers accountable in court.

Ultimately, while the Malhotras could have tried to hide behind the shield of diplomatic immunity in the Shanti Gurung case, they chose not to. In fact, they did not defend themselves at all, as they failed to respond to the original complaint or make any court appearances. They simply ignored the case, as well as the judgment against them, and Shanti has yet to receive the $1.5 million judgment owed to her. Despite this, with Adhikaar and the Urban Justice Center's support, Shanti has been connected to a better work situation, knows her rights and how to access resources, and is now leading a life free from abuse.

Access to Justice

Fortunately, as the case of Shanti Gurung shows, there is a network of resources available to assist trafficking victims and mistreated domestic workers. While many domestic workers can access these resources only if they are able to leave their abusive situation long enough to connect with someone from the outside world, recent years have brought a surge of activists and lawyers who are committed to aiding, empowering, and representing domestic workers.

One of the first avenues for relief for many domestic workers is the Trafficking Victims Protection Act (TVPA) of 2000 (subsequently reauthorized in 2003, 2008, and 2013).[40] The TVPA defines trafficking as follows:

> Sex trafficking in which a commercial sex act is induced by force, fraud, or coercion, or in which the person induced to perform such act has not attained 18 years of age; [or] the recruitment, harboring, transportation, provision, or obtaining of a person for labor or services, through the use of force, fraud, or coercion for the purpose of subjection to involuntary servitude, peonage, debt bondage, or slavery.[41]

The TVPA mandates that the State Department provide workers with a pamphlet explaining their rights and available resources in the event of exploitation. The law also gives consular officers discretion to evaluate whether a worker will face abuse in a given situation, and requires the State Department to record workers' arrivals and departures from the United States as well as allegations of abuse.[42] Along with the federal trafficking law, most states have enacted anti-trafficking legislation of their own, with New Jersey, Washington, California, New Mexico, and New York among the states with the most robust policies in place.[43]

To ensure they receive the legal protections of anti-trafficking legislation, domestic workers need the support and advocacy of community organizers and direct services providers. The power of the direct services model is best illustrated by the track record of the Institute for Policy Studies (IPS), a think tank that offers case management services for victims of trafficking. From 1997 to 2010, IPS assisted hundreds of trafficking victims, all of whom were domestic workers serving within the homes of diplomats.[44] Most of the workers were African, Southeast Asian, or South Asian immigrants—some of the most underserved, under-resourced, and under-networked of the domestic worker population. With funding from the Department of Health and Human Services authorized by the TVPA—as well as money from private foundations—IPS was able to connect workers to food, shelter, health care, and legal services for a thirteen-year period before staff departures in 2010 began to limit the group's ability to provide these services. By that time, other social work agencies had begun taking on this work. "We were running a social services agency out of a think tank," says Tiffany Williams, advocacy director of IPS's Break the Chain campaign, "but we had to: we were their only lifeline to the outside world."

Expanded direct services and advocacy networks on behalf of domestic workers and trafficked victims have helped more and more domestic workers to become aware of their rights and to bring cases against their abusive employers. Rocio Avila, an attorney with the Golden Gate University School of Law's Women's Employment Rights Clinic, represents domestic workers who sue for fair wages and overtime. Avila believes that these expanding resources, all with a presence on the Internet, enable more domestic workers to connect with advocates who can help them. Grassroots groups like the South Bay Coalition to End Human Trafficking (SBCEHT), for example, organize communities of domestic workers to inform them of their rights and the resources available to them. Along with SBCEHT, groups such as Mujeres Unidas y Activas and Filipino Advocates for Justice work in conjunction with law enforcement and legal services to aid trafficking victims. SBCEHT was able to connect Zoraida Pena Canal, an abused domestic worker, with Avila. "The power of the Internet, along with the potent domestic worker movement, actually connected this trafficking victim to social services and then to me," Avila says. "It's an ecosystem of law enforcement, advocates, social services providers, and physicians who help victims."[45] SBCEHT has a hotline for trafficking victims to access help as well. The National Domestic Workers Alliance, though primarily focused on ensuring labor protections for privately employed domestic workers, in 2013 began a campaign focused on addressing human trafficking[46]

Since advocates for trafficked domestic workers must work closely with law enforcement, there are groups whose purpose is to bridge the gap between domestic workers and the legal establishment. The Freedom Network, a national conglomeration of organizations, advocates, scholars, and attorneys, has long been an organizing force to aid trafficking victims. Ivy Suriyopas of the Asian American Legal Defense and Education Fund, who co-chairs the Freedom Network, says, "We crowd-source our knowledge and make vital connections; we rapidly respond to problems that we see," adding, "Domestic workers always walk through our doors. They work in homes, isolated; they are often the only employee in the entire household. They often have limited education or English; maybe they are vulnerable because of their immigration status. All of those factors can leave workers vulnerable, and in the wrong employer's household, it could lead to a trafficking situation."

In the context of legal services, a trafficking victim usually requires multiple types of advocacy—in particular, an immigration lawyer familiar with the T or U visa process. (A U visa enables victims of trafficking to remain in the United States legally while they pursue claims against their abusive employers, while a T visa permits human trafficking victims to remain in the country if they agree to testify against their employers.) In addition, the victim may pursue a civil case, which is the piece of the puzzle that Rocio Avila handles. "If they get deported, they can't pursue the criminal or civil matter," she says. "The federal trafficking statute is to ensure that the victim cooperates with law enforcement to be able to bring the perpetrator to justice."

To seek help, a worker first must escape his or her abusive employer with the assistance of an acquaintance or through connecting with a community organizer from an organization like SBCEHT. In Pena Canal's case, the employer, a successful real estate executive, brought Pena Canal to California from Peru to serve as a nanny and housekeeper. She kept Pena Canal working around the clock for no pay for two years. "No one expected this successful woman who worked in real estate would do this," says Avila. "But Pena Canal ended up confiding in parents at the school where she picked up the kids she cared for. The janitor at the school helped her, got the school secretary involved, and in a couple of months they built trust with her to convince her that she should leave." Before doing so, one of the parents at the school went online and found Domestic Workers United in New York; workers there told her to call Avila in San Francisco. Ultimately, Pena Canal was awarded over $600,000 for compensatory damages and emotional distress, and her abusive employer was sentenced to sixty months in prison. "The process of convincing the court of the above was itself a product of community lawyering and grassroots advocacy at its best," Avila says. "There is no way we could have prevailed if hadn't been for the groundbreaking work of the many individuals behind the domestic worker movement both in New York and in California, whom I used as my experts to educate the court and advocate for dignity for my client."

Despite the increased efforts of advocates and activists, many domestic workers still do not know their rights, or that the treatment they are receiving at the hands of abusive employers is a crime. Avila has observed that even workers whose cases do not rise to a trafficking charge live in fear of retaliation. "For the live-in nannies and housekeepers, the abuse I see is rampant. Employers are getting away with not even paying minimum wage. Most of my clients don't complain, out of fear: fear that their employer will turn against them, accuse them of stealing, call the cops. My clients live at the beck and call of their employers. I had one client whose employer would ring a bell, call her when they wanted an apple, water, tea. That doesn't always give rise to trafficking, but her situation is very bad, exploitative, devoid of dignity, not sustainable." Avila says that employers often tell her clients things like, "I can't pay you right now. If you leave, I will contact ICE and have you deported, and terrible things will happen to you."

To make matters even more challenging for trafficking victims, some of the resources meant to assist them were for years restricted by a contract between the Department of Health and

Human Services (HHS) and the National Conference of Catholic Bishops (NCCB). In 2006, HHS signed a contract with NCCB making the organization an intermediary between funding for TVPA and the organizations serving trafficked victims. However, NCCB did not allow advocates like IPS to provide any information about contraception or abortion.[47] "I had to tell the women who came to me during intake that contraception and abortion services would not be provided," recalls Tiffany Williams of the IPS. "During goal planning with the women who came to me, I had to state that we can't cover that information, the relationship between HHS and NCCB mandated that. Looking back on those interviews I wonder if I could have phrased it in another way so as not to preempt care these women could have received."[48]

The American Civil Liberties Union (ACLU) sued HHS over the contract, winning a judgment in Massachusetts Federal District Court saying that HHS had violated the Establishment Clause of the First Amendment to the Constitution by contracting with an entity that imposed its religious beliefs on trafficked people.[49] However, the First Circuit Court of Appeals vacated the ruling, holding that the federal government could still choose to contract with entities that refuse to offer reproductive health care to immigrant women who are victims of trafficking or who are detained by Homeland Security or are otherwise under government control. In her appellate brief to the First Circuit Court of Appeals, ACLU attorney Brigitte Amiri argued, "HHS has not come close to showing that it is absolutely clear that the circumstances giving rise to this case will not recur.... Furthermore, in addition to the TVPA contract, HHS has a long—and ongoing—history of contracting with [the Catholic Bishops] and accepting precisely the same abortion and contraception restrictions that are at the heart of this case.'"[50] When the contract between HHS and NCCB lapsed in 2011, the Obama administration did not renew it and instead went with a different intermediary, stating in its request for proposals that it would "have a strong preference" for groups that offered comprehensive health care.

"There Is Not as Much Help as There Is Need"

While many employers of domestic workers still view them as undeserving of equal employment rights, the current movement is working to change this viewpoint. The surge in activism over the past decade has raised consciousness among domestic workers and the general public. A former community organizer, Rocio Avila credits these activists with being a force for change in how domestic workers are able to access the resources they need to turn around their lives. This advocacy has engaged many diverse actors, from community organizers who live and work alongside domestic workers, to the highest leadership in the federal government, all of whom are "in motion around a shared vision," as National Domestic Workers Alliance director Ai-jen Poo has said.

There are numerous examples of government officials who are also allies of the movement; former labor secretary Hilda Solis, for example, who resigned her post in early 2013, pushed for minimum wage and overtime pay for domestic workers. Ultimately, though, it is today's advocates for domestic workers' rights who are helping to secure victories for domestic workers. Avila is a perfect example of this. Since graduating from law school in 2006, she has been representing domestic workers in Northern California in civil suits against abusive employers. Her clients have typically been denied the wages promised them, or even the legally mandated minimum wage. In the more egregious cases, her clients are human trafficking victims who have been physically or emotionally abused. All the work that she and her fellow activists have been doing on behalf of domestic workers and trafficking victims is still not enough, however; according to Avila, "There is not as much help as there is need."

2. "No Deal" for Domestic Workers: Activism Before, During, and After the New Deal

"A code for maids! I hope it fails. . . . I work far harder now than my maid does, and longer hours. Besides, no home that is a home, with children and frequent guests, can run strictly by the clock."—Mid-twentieth-century employer of domestic workers[1]

"We mean business this week or no washing." This was the no-nonsense message from laundry workers to their employers in Atlanta, Georgia, in 1881. The women had just formed the Atlanta Washing Society and announced that their members would strike unless given a raise to one dollar per dozen pounds of laundry.[2] Though the workers washed clothes inside of homes—sometimes inside their own homes—in isolation from other workers, the members of the Atlanta Washing Society evangelized their cause in churches, seeking solidarity among other washerwomen. (The group would grow to as many as three thousand members.)[3] Within three weeks of its formation, its demands unmet, the Atlanta Washing Society began a strike.

The city of Atlanta responded to the strike and the group's recruitment of new members by arresting and fining Washing Society members for disorderly conduct, taxing the group's membership, and encouraging local businesses to stop hiring women who belonged to the society.[4] Despite this pressure, the society pushed on, telling the city:

> We are determined to stand to our pledge and make extra charges for washing, and we have agreed and are willing

to pay $25 or $50 for licenses as a protection, so we can control the washing for the city. We can afford to pay these licenses, and will do it before we will be defeated, and then we will have full control of the city's washing at our own prices, as the city has control of our husbands' work at their prices. Don't forget this. We hope to hear from your council Tuesday morning. We mean business this week or no washing[5]

Eventually, the Atlanta city council rejected the idea of imposing fees on the society. Ultimately, as historian Tera W. Hunter of Princeton University has written, the strike resulted in "a greater appreciation for the fact that these women should not be taken for granted because of the role they played in the city's economy."[6]

In the decades that followed, domestic workers organized unions and associations to improve their working conditions and to generate solidarity. From 1870 to 1940, there were twenty domestic workers' unions affiliated with the American Federation of Labor, in various parts of the country.[7] Domestic workers also joined the Knights of Labor and the Industrial Workers of the World (IWW). One of the most successful efforts to unionize domestic workers during this time was led by Jane Street and the Domestic Workers' Industrial Union, IWW Local No. 113, founded in 1916 in Denver, Colorado. Street's vision for the union was larger than the traditional demands for better wages and shorter hours; she saw the union as a vehicle to "rebalance the power dynamic between mistress and servant." With its innovative strategies, including the creation of an alternative placement agency, the IWW Local made real gains in increasing wages and improving working conditions.[8] Similarly, in Harlem, New York, Dora Lee Jones created the Domestic Workers' Union, organizing seventy-five thousand African American domestic workers in the area.[9] The group secured a minimum wage of fifteen dollars per week and a maximum workday of ten hours. Jones's organizing inspired the formation of similar groups in New Jersey and Washington, DC.

One of the more well-known efforts of this period was that of the Young Women's Christian Association (YWCA). At the time, the notion that one couldn't find "good help" was becoming widespread. In response, the YWCA—comprised primarily of white, middle-class women who wanted to professionalize the industry rather than necessarily be worker advocates—sought, according to Hina Shah and Marci Seville of the Golden Gate University School of Law, to "re-conceptualize the mistress/maid relationship from a feudal one to a modern business contractual relationship, hoping to make the job more desirable for white working women."[10] The YWCA convened a national conference in 1928, which resulted in the formation of the National Council on Household Employment (NCHE), the goal of which was to "coordinate educational and research activities in the hopes of educating employers and workers, and to gradually work out standards for household employment."[11] The "code for maids" that the NCHE developed—which included overtime, paid time off, and limits on work hours—spread across the country during the 1930s and 1940s. The YWCA also attempted to bring domestic workers' issues to the attention of the Roosevelt administration, writing proposals to support New Deal protections for domestic workers. The National Recovery Administration, a preeminent New Deal agency, declined, stating that "the homes of individual citizens cannot be made the subject of regulations or restrictions and even if this were feasible, the question of enforcement would be virtually impossible."[12]

A major flaw in the YWCA's overall strategy was that its membership and leadership was not comprised of domestic workers. Instead, it was spearheaded by social workers and social scientists. In addition, the NCHE did not garner enough support among employers of domestic workers.[13] Though, according to Shah and Seville, the organization did begin to "[lay] the groundwork for justifying labor protection in the home as it changed the public's perception of the home as a place that could not be regulated and standardized," by 1945 the organization had fallen away.[14] Nevertheless, many of the YWCA's strategies and end goals are still relevant to today's movement, including the pursuit of overtime, days of rest, paid time off, and limits on work hours.[15]

The New Deal and the Exclusion of Domestic Workers

The New Deal ushered in a progressive ethical and legal framework for the treatment of the American worker, along with a host of federal and state laws regulating minimum wage, overtime, hiring practices, child labor policies, and other working conditions. Beginning with Franklin Delano Roosevelt's election as president in 1932 and ending in the early 1970s, the New Deal era was an outlier from the laissez-faire economics of the 1920s and the neoliberalism and economic deregulation that would follow it beginning in the 1980s.[16] William L. Niemi and David J. Plante of Western State College of Colorado argue:

> At its core, the New Deal regime aspired to a political economy with public (i.e., democratic) accountability in the financial system, in the corporate economy more generally, greater citizen equality with a real increase in life opportunities for the poor, women, and minorities (looking forward toward the politics of the 1960s), and hence, greater freedom as equal access to the political, economic, and cultural resources necessary to self-development.[17]

Unfortunately, the "life opportunities" the New Deal offered resulted mainly in protections for white workers. Most of the regulations explicitly or implicitly excluded domestic as well as agricultural workers, many of whom were African American. John P. Davis, founder of the National Negro Congress, testified before Congress in 1935 that the decision to exclude particular employees from New Deal legislation would leave black Americans helpless in the face of employers' abuses and discrimination:

> There is not a single thing [in the New Deal legislation] that will prevent the same type of ruthless exploitation of Negro workers.... [New Deal legislation] is supposed to be intended to help those workers whose lack of collective bargaining power renders them capable of exploitation by employers. As it stands, it does no such thing. . . . The economic crisis has not lifted for the Negro people. Because they are largely unskilled workers, reemployment for them has been slight. Negro domestic and agricultural laborers—representing the bulk of Negro labor—have had no benefits from the...protective legislation.[18]

Domestic workers even made a direct plea to Eleanor Roosevelt, when "Fifteen Weary Housemaids" wrote to the first lady about the Fair Labor Standards Act: "We have read in history books and other books about slavery of long ago, but the way the housemaids must work now from morning till night is too much for any human being. I think we girls should get some consideration as every other labor class has, even though it is housework."[19]

Thus, the New Deal's commitment to improving conditions for workers did not include all workers, but only a subset whose lives were deemed worthy of protection, regulation, and dignity. Examining two pillars of the New Deal, the National Labor Relations Act and the Fair Labor Standards Act, reveals how and why certain workers were excluded.

The National Labor Relations Act

In 1935, Congress passed the National Labor Relations Act (NLRA), which established the right of workers to organize, bargain collectively, and elect union representatives.[20] The law also established the National Labor Relations Board, a regulatory body that conducts elections for union representatives and investigates allegations of unfair labor practices.[21] Though politics have chipped away at its power and scope over the years, the NLRA continues to play an important role in protecting workers' ability to organize and collectively bargain.[22] However, from the beginning, the NLRA has excluded domestic workers.[23]

President Roosevelt did not want the NLRA to exclude any workers.[24] The first draft of the act, as introduced by Senator Robert Wagner, defined "employee" as "any person employed by an employer under any contract of hire, oral or written, express or implied, including all contracts entered into by helpers and assistants of employees, whether paid by employer or employee, if employed with the knowledge, actual or constructive, of the employer."[25] During hearings on the bill, Senator David Walsh of Massachusetts pointed out that the law would be challenging for farmers, as "it would permit an organization of employees who work on a farm, and would require the farmer to actually recognize their representatives, and deal with them in the matter of collective bargaining."[26] Subsequent drafts of the bill excluded agricultural and domestic labor, amending the language to state that "the term 'employee' shall include any employee . . . *but shall not include any individual employed as an agricultural laborer, or in the domestic service of any family or person at his home*" (emphasis added).[27] When the NLRA ultimately passed the Senate by a vote of sixty-three to twelve, agricultural and domestic workers were excluded from its protections.

This exclusion was the result of a deal struck between Roosevelt and legislators from the Southern states. Roosevelt knew that passage of the NLRA and other New Deal legislation required the support of Southern politicians, which was contingent on the ability of the region's political economy to continue without limitation—in other words, on the continued supply of the cheap labor of black Americans. The compromise position between FDR and Southern politicians was, in the words of Juan F. Perea of the Loyola University of Chicago School of Law, "race-neutral language that both accommodated the southern desire to exclude blacks but did not alienate northern liberals nor blacks in the way that an explicit racial exclusion would."[28] In the mid-1930s, most black workers in the South were engaged in either domestic work or farm labor. Excluding both types of work from the NLRA guaranteed that these workers could not form unions, reinforcing a racial regime of white domination, and a labor regime of extreme exploitation.

The legislative history of the NLRA does not show overt evidence of racial prejudice. Rather, it reveals concern about the administrative difficulty of extending coverage to agricultural and domestic workers.[29] However, Perea argues that this history does in fact have clear racial overtones, and that this racial discrimination renders the NLRA unconstitutional. Evidence of the racial component, he says, is in the exclusion itself: the law could have exempted small businesses, including farms, but instead explicitly excluded specific classes of employees, a decision rooted in Southern legislators' desire to maintain the economic way of life of the region, which depended on continued exploitation of the African American worker. Though slavery was unconstitutional after the passage of the Thirteenth Amendment in 1865, the exploitation of black workers continued for decades in both domestic and agricultural labor, as it was considered essential to the Southern economy.

According to Perea, the NLRA aimed to protect workers' attempts to bargain collectively mainly for the purpose of avoiding strikes and their resulting costs to business. (The NLRA legislative history notes that over a two-year period, thirty-two million working days were lost to strikes.[30]) Thus, the real objective of the NLRA was to equalize bargaining power between wage earners and large industrialists, in order to avoid strikes and the resulting disruption of the national economy. But the NLRA set an unfortunate precedent: the exclusion of domestic workers became consistent through all labor legislation of the New Deal era.

Fair Labor Standards Act

In 1938, Congress passed the Fair Labor Standards Act (FLSA), which required a minimum wage, maximum working hours, and overtime pay for workers. Although FLSA ended regional wage differences and began the process of standardizing the way most employees were treated under the law, it applied a narrow interpretation of the Commerce Clause to exclude numerous employees either explicitly, like agricultural workers, or implicitly, like domestic workers.[31] Since private enterprise was not seen as affecting interstate commerce, and domestic work was considered a purely private enterprise, Shah and Seville explain, "domestic work was seen as not affecting interstate commerce…and thus the work was originally considered as not part of FLSA's coverage."[32]

Like the NLRA, the FLSA excluded domestic workers primarily because Southern legislators wanted to keep wages for black Americans low, with one legislator stating that "agricultural laborers have been explicitly excluded from participation in any of the benefits of New Deal legislation...for the simple and effective reason that it has been deemed politically certain that their inclusion would have spelled death of the legislation in Congress."[33] Unlike the NLRA, FLSA's discriminatory intent was much more open and apparent. During the hearings on the legislation, Senator "Cotton" Ed Smith of South Carolina complained about the decay of America as a result of the introduction of African Americans into political society, saying, "I shall not attempt to use the proper adjective to designate, in my opinion, this bill [the FLSA]! Any man on this floor who has sense enough to read the English language knows that the main object of this bill is, by human legislation, to overcome the splendid gifts of God to the South."[34]

The concept of equal pay as established by FLSA was just too radical for this era's racial politics. Enforcing equal pay would have put workers of color on equal footing with white workers.[35] Representative J. Mark Wilcox of Florida stated: "You cannot put the Negro and the white man on the same [economic] basis and get away with it. Not only would such a situation result in grave social and racial conflicts but it would also result in throwing the Negro out of employment and in making him a public charge. There just is not any sense in intensifying this racial problem in the South, and this bill cannot help but produce such a result."[36]

Thus, domestic workers were wholly left out of the first major worker protections the United States had ever seen. The exclusion was so clearly rooted in both racism and sexism that the entanglement of both in rendering domestic work invisible under the law is deeply evident.

Post-New Deal Domestic Worker Policy and Activism

During the mid-part of the twentieth century, pockets of domestic worker activism remained but did not emerge as a major force in the civil rights movement. Preeminent legislation of the era such as the Civil Rights Act of 1964 barred discrimination in employment but applied only to employers of fifteen or more people.[37] This naturally excluded households, as most would not employ that many nannies or caregivers. The Occupational Safety and Health Act and the Age Discrimination in Employment Act included similar employee-number thresholds.[38]

Though activism was less widespread overall, there were some fierce advocates during the late 1960s and 1970s, including the California Homemakers Association and the National Domestic Workers Union founded in Atlanta by Dorothy Bolden, as well as many tenacious New York union activists.[39] And it was a New York legislator who paved the way for the most important domestic worker policy of the post–New Deal era, when Bronx state assemblyman Seymour Posner began advocating in 1974 to include domestic workers as part of the state's minimum wage law—foretelling the critical role of New York in today's movement.

One federal policy achievement did occur in 1974, when Congress finally amended the Fair Labor Standards Act to include domestic workers within minimum wage protections.[40] Feminist activists like Edith Barksdale Sloan, Shirley Chisholm, and Bella Abzug had pressed the issue in Congress.[41] Their influence on Congress's thinking at this time is reflected in statements such as one by the male chair of the US House of Representatives Committee on Education and Labor: "Extending minimum wage and overtime protection to domestic service workers will not only raise the wages of these workers but will improve the sorry image of household employment.... Including domestic workers under the protection of the Act should help to raise the status and dignity of this work."[42]

But this victory was limited, as during the same year, the Department of Labor enacted a regulation that exempted home care companions hired directly by families, as well as companions hired by third-party employers, from earning minimum wage and overtime.[43] The belief behind these partial inclusions was that care labor was, according to Shah and Seville, a "pleasurable side activity done to supplement income rather than a viable profession for many low-income minority women."[44] As Eileen Boris, professor of feminist studies at University of California Santa Barbara, and Jennifer Klein, professor of history at Yale University, have pointed out, conservative business interests were adamant about the exclusion of home care workers, as part of an across-the-board pushback on any type of gains for labor.[45] The exclusion was sustained for decades: as recently as 2007, the Supreme Court upheld this companionship exemption as valid and binding in the case of *Long Island Care v. Home, Ltd.* Under former Labor Secretary Hilda Solis's leadership, and with President Obama's backing, the Department of Labor finally reformed the companionship exemption in 2013.

Other than securing FLSA protections for a narrow slice of the domestic workforce, domestic worker activism did not begin to produce positive changes to state or federal policy or sustained organization among workers until the 1990s—in part because of resistance from the U.S labor movement. One vibrant global effort was the International Wages for Housework Campaign, which was founded in 1972 by Selma James and still exists today. James argued, "To the degree that we organize a struggle for wages for the work we do in the home, we demand that work in the home be considered as work which, like all work in capitalist society, is forced work, which we do not for love but because, like every other worker, we and our children would starve if we stopped."[46]

This campaign, which James organized along with Mariarosa Dalla Costa, demanded that the government compensate work that took place inside the home. This idea was met with scorn not only by politicians, but also within the labor movement. Labor unions did not see the struggle of domestic workers as part of the "real" labor movement and, according to James, unions actually worked to "maintain unequal rates of pay" for women. She believed that unions did nothing in the way of addressing women's concerns about labor, and how it was valued in the broader economy, in part because they repeated the patterns of capital markets.[47] She wrote:

> The union *prevents* such organization, by following organizationally the way capital is organized: a fragmented class, divided into those who have wages and those who don't. The unemployed, the old, the ill, children, and housewives are unwaged. So the unions ignore us and thereby separate us from each other and from the waged…. But for those of us who are deprived of wages for our work, who are full-time housewives and do not have jobs outside the home, unions don't know we exist. When capital pays husbands they get two workers, not one.[48]

The 1980s were characterized by President Ronald Reagan's efforts at "removing the government's smothering hand," meaning more freedom for business (as well as a reduction in social programs) and less power for workers.[49] At the same time, Reagan-era initiatives began to change the face of the home care sector. In 1981, the federal Medicaid budget enabled states to use their Medicaid dollars to support home-based long-term care.[50] This led to a surge in in-home care workers—and concomitant organizing of these workers by unions like the Service Employees International Union.

Today, the domestic workers' movement's ability to make progress has much to do with American labor's ideological evolution, as well as shifts in power to domestic workers themselves. These changes are evident in what happened in New York in the lead-up to the passage of the Domestic Workers' Bill of Rights in 2010.

3. Triumph in New York

"If the domestic workers went on strike, the whole city would shut down."—**Councilwoman Gale Brewer,** sponsor of New York City domestic workers' legislation[1]

"The Domestic Workers' Bill of Rights will bring dignity, respect, and long overdue legal protections to essential care givers across this state…. I commend the members of Domestic Workers United for their tireless efforts to raise awareness and focus public attention on the needs of this often invisible workforce. This bill rights a wrong that began when domestic workers were excluded from the labor protections created by the New Deal and brings us one step closer to our goal of dignity and fairness for all workers across this state."—**New York Assembly Speaker Sheldon Silver**, who originally refused to bring the Domestic Workers' Bill of Rights to a vote on the Assembly floor[2]

Born in Barbados, Barbara Young came to the United States nearly twenty years ago at the age of forty-six. In Barbados, Young had worked as a bus conductor, where she was also a union organizer.[3] However, her job had been eliminated due to restructuring policies. "'Restructuring' meant laying off nine hundred forty-three bus conductors," Young recalls. "And this was a great job. I had benefits. But after the layoff I was unable to support myself or my family. It was a time of fear and anger for me and many other people."

After six months of looking for a job in Barbados without success, Young decided to move to the United States, joining her daughter who already lived in New York. She became a live-in nanny, working for a couple with a thirteen-month-old son. Young lived at her employers' home from Tuesday through Saturday. "I ended up demanding Saturdays off," Young said. "At first the couple resisted, but I had had enough of staying with the family all day on Saturdays when they never even went anywhere. Then on Saturday nights, the child's parents would stay out until 2:00 a.m. and I would be at home with the baby. They'd send me home at 2:00 a.m. I'd be on the subway going back to Queens at 2:00 a.m.!" Only after she threatened to quit did the family agree to let her have Saturdays off.

Even as she tangled with her employers, Young developed a bond with the boy she was caring for. "He was so close to me," she reminisced. "Even today I think of him, though I'm not in contact with his family. I remember that when he got his brown belt in karate, it was such a victory for him—and afterward he ran straight to me. He gave me a hug and asked me, 'Are you proud of me, Barbara?' In everything he did, he wanted to make me proud."

The bond that develops between domestic workers and those in their care can make it challenging for workers to assert their rights. But Young continued to speak up, asking her employers to deduct Social Security payments from her paycheck. They agreed, but instead of depositing that money into the Social Security system, at the end of the year they gave her back all the money they had deducted in cash. "They just kept giving me deductions in cash," she said. "But I wanted to be able to work and save like a regular person." Because of this, Young left the family after working for them for seven years.

She then accepted a live-in nanny job in lower Manhattan.

During this time, Young obtained a certificate from Hunter College's Community Organizing and Development program, and started attending meetings of Domestic Workers United (DWU). Young began recruiting members to join DWU, approaching workers wherever she encountered them—in libraries, on the subway. Because of her strong public speaking and organizing abilities, her colleagues in the movement came to call her "the mayor." "Barbara is somebody who I think would be incredible to have serving in public office," Ai-jen Poo, director of the National Domestic Workers Alliance, says. "Hers is the kind of leadership for a new America that I think is needed."

It was domestic workers like Barbara Young who were critical to the passage of New York's Domestic Workers' Bill of Rights. Enacted in 2010, it was the first law in the United States to establish statutory employment protections for domestic workers. The legislation guaranteed overtime, paid rest days, and meal and rest breaks for domestic workers—an astounding victory for domestic workers and their advocates in light of the historic exclusion of domestic work from such protections. Governor David Paterson's signature on the bill was the culmination of a decade-long campaign led by the New York Domestic Workers' Justice Coalition, which was comprised of an impressive multiethnic and multicultural array of groups including DWU, Adhikaar for Human Rights and Social Justice, Cidadao Global, Hispanic Resource Center, Las Mujeres de Santa Maria, New Immigrant Community Empowerment, Unity Housecleaners, Damayan Migrant Workers Association, Haitian Women for Haitian Refugees, and Andolan Organizing South Asian Workers.

In social movements, a specific victory is usually the end result of years of organizing, strategizing, coalition building, demonstrating, meeting, writing, and tenacious pounding of the pavement. All of these were present in the New York domestic workers' rights campaign. A key moment was the formation of DWU in 2000 by members of two Asian immigrant community organizations, the Committee Against Anti-Asian Violence and Andolan: Organizing South Asian Workers. Initially, the organization worked in a few neighborhoods in New York City with large Asian populations. Eventually, DWU began to recruit Latino, African, and Caribbean workers, turning it into "an industry-based multiethnic organization."[4]

"It was a vibrant and close-knit community of women who were excited about finally having a home for domestic workers to address their needs," former DWU executive director Priscilla Gonzalez recalls. "Even though it was a multiethnic organization, these women's primary identity was about being workers. One element of the stories they shared among each other was the severe power imbalance between them and their employers; they felt expendable but also threatened, severely poorly paid, and that their work was not valued."[5]

At the time of DWU's formation, domestic workers in New York had no guarantee of days off, protection from harassment, or disability or workers' compensation.[6] Domestic workers deemed "companions" were excluded from receiving a minimum wage and overtime protections, and live-in domestic workers were excluded from overtime.[7] Adding to the structural barriers domestic workers faced, employment agencies were in many instances colluding with individual employers to exploit workers, and job assignments for domestic workers did not have to include clear expectations.

In response, DWU and other groups secured legislation in 2003 that required employment agencies to inform nannies and other live-in workers in writing about their responsibilities, wages, and expected hours. Families who employed domestic workers had to sign an agreement stating that they were aware of their workers' rights regarding minimum wage, overtime pay, and Social Security.[8] Three years later, legislation also passed in Nassau County, Long Island, requiring that employment agencies give domestic workers contract forms and notices of their rights, like minimum wage, overtime regulations, and Social Security.[9] Members of UNITY, a domestic housecleaning cooperative, worked to enact the Nassau County law.[10]

In 2003, DWU also held its first "Having Your Say" Convention, gathering over two hundred domestic workers from more than a dozen different home countries.[11] Despite differences in language and custom, the workers found commonalities in that they had all toiled for employers who did not respect basic labor standards. Conference attendees responded to a survey about their working conditions and conversed at tables about their shared experiences. The conversations produced a list of demands including overtime pay, meal and rest breaks, a day of rest, and a few days of paid time off per year. These demands formed the basis of a state bill for domestic worker rights, which was first introduced in the State Assembly in 2004.[12] "When I joined [DWU] in 2003," Priscilla Gonzalez recalls, "the organized workers were beginning to set their sights on changing labor law—and labor law gets changed not at the city level but at the state level, which is a whole other political terrain."

DWU worked with Assemblyman Keith Wright of Harlem, who was planning to introduce his own bill to protect domestic workers' rights. After Wright met with workers and advocates, he decided to introduce DWU's bill instead. At this stage, DWU had already begun to organize workers' trips to Albany to meet with legislative members and their aides, as well as holding rallies and press conferences. Unfortunately, this bill died in what Barbara Ehrenreich called "the notoriously comatose state legislature."[13]

Employer Groups: Crucial New York Coalition Member

Legal scholar and Yale law professor Reva Siegel writes that social movements are subject to the "public value condition," which means they must frame their themes and express their convictions as "public values."[14] The domestic workers' movement's success in New York illustrates Siegel's argument, as workers effectively appealed to the broader population, including families who employed domestic workers. One of the events most critical to securing support from New York employers was a meeting between National Domestic Workers' Alliance director Ai-jen Poo and Jews for Racial and Economic Justice (JFREJ). Poo came to JFREJ's offices, spoke about the domestic workers' movement, and encouraged JFREJ to get involved. This meeting took place in 2002, as the movement for legislation in New York was heating up. Recalls Rachel McCullough, the current organizer of JFREJ's domestic workers' effort, "JFREJ had to do some internal soul searching and really figure it out: How would we organize employers?" JFREJ's board ultimately decided to take on the issue.[15]

To persuade their members and others in the Jewish community to get involved, JFREJ attempted to connect the issue of domestic workers to historical Jewish struggles. Gayle Kirshenbaum, a mother and longtime progressive political activist and a member of JFREJ, became one of the most visible members of the employer movement. In her conversations, Kirshenbaum compared modern-day Latina, African, Asian, and South Asian domestic workers to Jewish garment workers, and their struggle for labor rights, at the turn of the twentieth century. "Jewish women garment workers were among the first organized workers," Kirshenbaum says. "The people who come into our homes have the same motivations as our Jewish ancestors did."[16]

Kirshenbaum had just had her first child at the time, and had gone through the experience of hiring a nanny. She recalls that she expected her son's nanny to come to the job and tell her what the terms of employment would be, but this turned out not to be the case. "I wish I had known more and taken responsibility for knowing more about what that relationship would be like," she says. Kirshenbaum spoke at her synagogue about her experience hiring and working with her child's caregiver. "It was personally radical to bring a private struggle of hiring a nanny into the public domain," she said. "After my speech a lot of people came up to me to talk about their struggles."

Kirshenbaum and JFREJ began by creating a model contract for employers to use in their hiring of domestic employees. However, that strategy promptly fell on its face. "We realized we needed to start ten steps back, to talk about why this is important," Kirshenbaum said. So JFREJ and Kirshenbaum started the One Step Up campaign, which encouraged employers to make small changes to their relationships with their caregivers. "We said to people, 'If you're not offering paid sick days now for your nanny or caregiver, start by just doing that. Can you do that?'" Kirshenbaum remembers. "It was baby steps." The JFREJ also began a series of events called the Living Room Project, where employers of domestic workers would gather in one another's homes and discuss issues relating to the hiring of care workers and how those workers' rights could best be protected.

The Living Room Project and the One Step Up campaign ultimately led to the formation of the Employers for Justice Network, and then Hand in Hand, an organization focused exclusively on organizing employers around domestic workers' rights and issues. Eventually, employers in New York who were exposed to JFREJ and the Domestic Workers Alliance's activism began to join domestic workers on trips to Albany to lobby state legislators—a transformative activity in itself. Traveling together and speaking alongside one another dramatically changed the relationship between workers and employers.[17] Once formed, this relationship became, as Ai-jen Poo explained in her essay "Organizing with Love," one of the most important of the New York campaign:

> Campaigns that bring people together to make positive change in the world, like the Bill of Rights Campaign, are ideal vessels for assumptions and values such as ours. These principles served as the basis for one of our most important alliances, our relationship with the Shalom Bayit project of Jews for Racial and Economic Justice (JFREJ). Shalom Bayit—which means "peace in the home" in Hebrew—was the name of JFREJ's project to organize a network of domestic employers, "Employers for Justice."[18]

Another coalition partner who contributed extensively to the New York campaign—particularly in the final stages—was Adhikaar, a nonprofit that works in Nepali communities. "Our focus is mostly New York, educating members so they know about the law and, more importantly, using the state law as a tool to build leadership, train, teach about negotiation skills, do outreach in community," Adhikaar's director, Luna Ranjit, says. "We were the first forum for Nepali-speaking domestic workers."[19]

The organization launched in 2005 and immediately got involved in the domestic workers' campaign. "Our participation in the process helped build the leadership of a lot of our members," Ranjit says. "The bill itself is a wonderful victory, especially for new people to this country." In particular, Adhikaar ramped up its activism during the home stretch of the campaign, when other groups had grown weary. "We were very active toward the end," Ranjit states. "We went to Albany a lot, and we were active in mobilizing for all the New York City actions."

According to Ranjit, the organizing in New York had two powerful factors in its favor: broad support, and timing: "Having support across the board among employers of domestic workers, unions, elected officials actively championing it, was important. The political climate was also right. Also, there was no active opposition in New York." In the wake of the bill, Ranjit is optimistic about what the future holds. "I'm excited about the change in consciousness among workers and employers," she says. "It's a slow process. The *New York Times* still uses the term 'maid,' for example, but it's slowly changing. Some of our members now have contracts, they know how to negotiate, and employers are beginning to change. Laws are a tool to inspire that change."

The Closer

While the advocates and community organizers at the heart of the New York Domestic Workers' Justice Coalition pounded the pavement throughout the state, a key player did his work inside the halls of the capitol. In December 2007, DWU decided to bring in a professional lobbyist. Ed Ott, executive director of the New York City Central Labor Council, arranged for DWU representatives, including Poo and Haeyoung Yoon, an attorney with the National Employment Law Project, to meet with Richard Winsten, a longtime lobbyist for labor unions. As Winsten recalls, Poo and Yoon told him: "We've been working on this Bill of Rights legislation and can't seem to get any traction with it in Albany... If you could give us some suggestions, advise us, work with us, see whether anything might be possible?"[20] Impressed by Poo and Yoon, as well as Ott's endorsement, Winsten agreed to represent DWU pro bono.

Successfully recruiting Winsten was the end result of a long-term cultivation of organized labor by the domestic workers' movement. "At the beginning, we were laughed out of meetings for thinking we could change labor law at a time when workers' rights were being increasingly curtailed across the country," former DWU director Priscilla Gonzalez recalls.[21] "But there was always this sense of respect for our attempt, and the fact that this was led by immigrant women and women of color." According to Gonzalez, domestic workers reminded many male labor leaders of their own mothers. She points out that John Sweeney, who was the head of the AFL-CIO at the time, traveled to Albany specifically to work on domestic workers' legislation. He talked about how his mother had been a domestic worker and how proud he was to be able to do right by her so many decades later. "The wives, mothers, and grandmothers of many mainstream union members were actually domestic workers," Gonzalez says. "So there was a very organic connection just on that level among the unions and our domestic workers."

Winsten began meeting with legislative leaders. It immediately became clear to him that the movement's strongest arguments were those rooted in the need to obtain legal parity with other labor provisions such as minimum wage and overtime, and that the more difficult requests were those for benefits that went beyond parity. In particular, Winsten perceived that the demand for employer-provided health insurance was inhibiting the bill's progress. He explained to DWU's leadership that the health insurance provisions were "nonstarters" but insisted, "We can accomplish very important things if you're willing to go down this road with me, one of which is the legal parity route."[22]

Winsten knew that the support of New York State assembly speaker Sheldon Silver was critical. However, Silver initially expressed concerns about some aspects of the legislation. "When

I first spoke with him directly," Winsten recalls, "he was really clear on the point that he thinks domestic workers should be treated equally but it's more difficult and costly to mandate health protections via the state legislature. But overtime, days of rest, coverage of disability laws or human rights laws, that he was one hundred percent supportive of." Silver also had mixed feelings about domestic workers gaining collective bargaining rights. Winsten pointed out that domestic workers, like farmworkers, had always been excluded from the National Labor Relations Act. "This is a Jim Crow exclusion," Winsten said. "As we came closer to succeeding in the assembly," he remembers, "Silver was very clear he was willing to pass a bill that ended the exclusion from collective bargaining, but that collective bargaining would be logistically difficult." Still, Winsten was confident the coalition could ultimately gain Silver's full support: "Look, Silver has a lengthy track record for being an advocate for working people and particularly the working poor during his tenure as speaker of the assembly in New York. He has consistently supported wage theft legislation, and he represents the Lower East Side, which was the cradle of the New Deal–era labor and Social Security legislation."

Winsten also interfaced with the two legislators who sponsored the bill, Assemblyman Keith Wright—who had introduced the original domestic workers' bill—and Diane Savino of the New York State Senate. Wright's family included domestic workers, so he was well aware of the historic exclusion of domestic workers from labor protections. Savino had long been sympathetic to the rights of workers and a strong advocate for women's rights, so she was an ideal sponsor in the senate.

All the advocacy in the world cannot achieve policy change, however, unless the political conditions are hospitable. Fortunately, the stars aligned for New York's Domestic Workers' Bill of Rights. First, in 2009, Democrats gained control of the state senate for the first time in almost half a century. In addition, after Eliot Spitzer was forced to step down as governor after an embarrassing sex scandal in 2008, Winsten correctly surmised that his successor, David Paterson, "would be interested in doing something to end this discrimination against domestic workers." In the beginning, however, the tone from Paterson's office was negative. "He said we can't mandate a wage raise, can't mandate health insurance," Winsten recalls. "He said middle-class people employ domestics, and we have to worry about driving up costs to that group. So yes, there was skepticism from the governor's office." Despite his initial misgivings, Paterson ultimately signed the bill. "He grew up in the labor and civil rights movement," Winsten says. "He ultimately got it."

Floor debate on the New York law reveals how other legislators grappled with the fact that domestic work actually is work. For example, in the debate over vacation days, Democratic assemblyman Keith Wright explained to Republican assemblyman David Townsend that when a domestic worker accompanies her employers to Disneyland for a family vacation, she is still "at work":

> Mr. Townsend: Okay. If the family that employs the domestic worker goes on vacation, say, to Florida, to Disney World, and takes their domestic worker with them, does that count towards their vacation time?

> Mr. Wright: No, that's part of their employment. That's actually a part of their employment and, in fact, many domestic workers do go on family vacations, whether it's during Christmas, whether it's during Martin Luther King holiday, Thanksgiving, what have you. They do

go on vacations, but it's not a vacation for the domestic worker; in fact, many of them leave their own families, to the detriment of their own families; then they have to work during these holidays when they go on spring break, let's say, to Disney World.

Mr. Townsend: So, what you're saying is if they go to Disney World, they're not free to—you're like me, hard to hear—they're not free to go on their own to visit whatever sites they want?

Mr. Wright: No. They're, in fact, working. They are working. They are working. If the family is going on vacation, they're vacationing and enjoying themselves, but these domestic workers are, in fact, working.[23]

Townsend, who had voted against the legislation in previous years, supported the 2010 bill.

In the New York State Senate, the bill passed on June 2, 2010, by a vote of 33 to 28.[24] The vote in the New York Assembly on July 1, 2010, was 104 in favor to 39 against.[25] While the political makeup of the state senate and the governor's office obviously mattered, it was the persistence and consistence of the activists on the ground that ultimately led to the law's passage. "What DWU did particularly well was to be positioned to take advantage of those breaks when they came," Winsten says, "because they had done all of their homework and organizing work and lobbying training work, [which] you need to do to effectively take advantage of those moments." Winsten also credits the black, Latino, and Asian caucuses. "Most of those members, they may have had someone in their family who was a domestic worker. And even for white members of the legislature who gravitated to the law—maybe they had experiences themselves as domestic workers or with domestic workers in their family. Ultimately this became very relatable to many members of the legislature."

However, Winsten reserves his highest praise for Ai-jen Poo and the other leaders of the movement. "I'm in awe of them. They're doing the job that most other people would've considered impossible to do because of all the legal, logistical, practical difficulties of it and given all the immense obstacles they face. These are extraordinary intellects and organizers. It's a rare combination to find. If we had twenty of them maybe the whole labor movement wouldn't be reeling as badly as it is."

Provisions and Enforcement

The Domestic Workers' Bill of Rights went into effect on November 29, 2010, closing gaps in the state's labor laws that had left domestic workers with fewer rights than other workers. While domestic workers—both those employed by private households and those employed by agencies—had long been covered by state minimum wage rules, overtime provisions, and other workplace laws, many were exempt, while others were subject to lower overtime standards. The Bill of Rights was an important step in narrowing these exemptions; three years later, federal labor regulations approved by President Obama went even further in protecting all US domestic workers.

Overall, the New York law's provisions include:

1. **Expanded minimum wage coverage:** The law extended minimum wage coverage to part-time babysitters, except those employed on a casual basis (meaning they work irregularly), and to live-in companions. These two groups of workers had previously been exempted from minimum wage provisions.[26]

2. Expanded overtime coverage: Live-out domestic workers who work more than forty hours per week and live-in domestic workers and companions who work more than forty-four hours per week were now entitled to the higher overtime rate that applies to most other workers in the state. (Agency-employed companions were entitled to overtime at time-and-one-half minimum wage before passage of the Bill of Rights, and continue to have that overtime entitlement.)[27]

3. Day of rest and three annual leave days: The bill adds to New York's existing "One Day Rest in Seven" provision, granting domestic workers a day of rest each week and providing overtime pay if they voluntarily work on their day of rest. The law also grants domestic workers three days of leave after one year of employment with the same employer. Workers employed for at least twenty hours but fewer than thirty hours per week are entitled to two days. Workers employed for thirty hours or more per week are entitled to the full three days.[28]

4. Workplace protection: New York's Human Rights Law did not previously protect domestic workers because it defined "employee" to exclude domestic workers, and "employer" to exclude employers with fewer than four employees. The bill removed those two exemptions and added a new section to the Human Rights Law specifically prohibiting sexual harassment and harassment on the basis of race, religion, or national origin by domestic employers. [29]

5. Change in disability benefits: The law removed, from the definitions section of New York's Disability Benefits

Law, the exception for "domestic or personal worker in a private home who is employed for less than forty hours per week by any one employer," and added "domestic or personal work in a private home" to the definition of "employment."[30]

Despite its substantial accomplishments, among the things the bill did not include were paid sick days, paid personal days, paid vacation days, advance notice of termination, and severance pay.[31] Instead of including these benefits, the New York State Legislature asked the state Department of Labor to complete a study on the feasibility of domestic workers' collectively bargaining for these gains. Coalition members also wanted, but were unable to secure, notice of termination for domestic workers—or, in lieu of notice, compensation. "It is too bad that this provision was not included, ultimately," Haeyoung Yoon of the National Employment Law Project says, "as it is very important for live-in domestic workers to know if they risk being terminated. When you live with your employer, and you're summarily fired, you risk becoming homeless."

Since passage of the bill in 2010, domestic workers' groups have been grappling with how best to educate both domestic workers and employers about the new labor protections. It hasn't been easy. In April 2011, the *New York Times* published a piece arguing that few New York nannies were aware of the law: "More than seven months after the bill was signed into law with some fanfare, most domestic workers and their employers seem unaware of it, and its impact on the often-fluid business arrangements between the two groups appears to have been negligible, say nannies, labor advocates, state officials and others."[32] Sharon Lerner wrote in the *Nation* in June 2012 that "penalties for [domestic worker abuse] are still few and far between. Since November 2010, when the law went into effect, and mid-February of 2012, only five complaints had been brought to resolution."[33]

In 2011, a group of employers based in Park Slope, Brooklyn, called Park Slope Parents conducted a series of nanny compensation surveys that included feedback from over one thousand area parents.[34] The survey revealed that on average nannies were paid between $14.22 and $16.32 per hour, depending on how many children were in their care. (Nannies who were paid off the books earned slightly higher salaries on average.) The survey also revealed a positive trend about paid leave in Brooklyn: nearly 80 percent of surveyed parents paid their nannies regular wages while they were away. On the negative side, however, 44 percent of employers still did not pay their nannies overtime, even though the overtime requirement was one of the most groundbreaking aspects of the New York law.[35] Sixty-three percent reported paying their nannies off the books, even though the requirement to pay on the books has always been in place in New York.

In addition, that the volume of worker abuse cases hasn't changed in the wake of the new legislation is a concern. According to Hollis Pfitsch of the Legal Aid Society of New York, "We continue to be frustrated at the amount of 'one-off' cases we do, which settle with a confidentiality order and do not necessarily have any direct impact on changing the rampant exploitation of domestic workers. To that end, in addition to cases which come to us through our general intake processes, we also take cases for members of domestic worker organizations like Domestic Workers United, Adhikaar, and Damayan. The clients who are referred to us by these worker centers are usually engaged in speaking out about their experience to some extent and our successes in those cases therefore have more impact on the larger problem."[36]

While widespread compliance will take time to ensure, the New York legislation does provide clarity and guidance where none previously existed. Breedlove, an Austin-based company that for twenty years has offered financial services and guidance in payroll taxes and other regulations related to caregivers, sees the highly practical upside to the bill of rights. "One function of the state law is that it offers specificity above and beyond the federal law," says Stephanie Breedlove, the company's co-founder and a mother of two sons. "The legislation is a real win-win, because it makes it easier for the employer and the caregiver to understand the parameters of the relationship."[37] Breedlove's New York clientele has increased by 25 percent since the law was enacted in 2010, and among her clients, few express concerns about the cost of complying with the new wage provisions. "The fact is, affording care is expensive. I think the hardest struggle families had even before laws came about is affording care, period."

Passing the New York Domestic Workers' Bill of Rights was a journey that stretched ten years. Beyond changing labor law, the decade-long campaign leveraged the leadership abilities of the women who comprise the domestic worker sector, and furthered the movement for dignity and respect for all workers. "Our movement is about *every* low-wage worker," Priscilla Gonzalez says. "We crafted very intentionally broad messages that could appeal to a lot of different kinds of people. Everybody deserves to be treated with dignity on the job."

4. Heartbreak in California

"He vetoed the bill, but he can't take away everything we have learned. We are ready for our next campaign."
—**Enma Delgado**, Mujeres Unidas y Activas

Director Ai-jen Poo of the National Domestic Workers Alliance believes social justice campaigns are analogous to great love stories. "I often compare great campaigns to great love affairs because they're an incredible container for transformation." Poo says. "You can change policy, but you also change relationships and people in the process."[1] Unfortunately, many love stories end in heartbreak. On September 30, 2012, Poo and her fellow organizers at NDWA had their hearts broken when California governor Jerry Brown vetoed the state's Domestic Workers' Bill of Rights, AB 889.

The bill had passed the California legislature several weeks prior, and with a staunch progressive like Brown in the governor's office, Poo and her fellow domestic worker advocates were hopeful it would become law. For nearly a decade, NDWA had been working on passing this bill, which would have required labor protections for California's mostly female and foreign-born domestic worker population. (Of the estimated 217,000 domestic workers in California, almost 70 percent are Latina, and an overwhelming 93 percent are women.)[2] "We cover baristas, parking attendants in labor laws," California state senator Tom Ammiano, a fierce champion of the legislation, said. "But these women are the last group that's still left out of labor law."[3]

Like its companion legislation in New York, the California

Domestic Workers' Bill of Rights would have required overtime pay, adequate sleeping conditions for live-in workers, and meal and rest breaks—protections domestic workers have historically never received. The California legislation pushed a bit further than New York's by seeking the use of kitchen facilities and a specific number of hours of uninterrupted sleep for live-in workers, as well as workers' compensation. (Lack of adequate food and sleep and on-the-job injuries have been noted as problems for domestic workers.)[4] The 2012 legislation was actually the second time California had failed to pass a Domestic Workers' Bill of Rights; the first bill, in 2006, had been vetoed by then governor Arnold Schwarzenegger.[5]

The movement for domestic workers' legislation in California actively began in 2003, but as in New York, immigrant community organizers in California had long been laying the groundwork for a Domestic Workers' Bill of Rights.[6] Among these groups was Mujeres Unidas y Activas (Women United and Active; MUA), a grassroots organization for Latina immigrants in San Francisco, founded in 1990. With over four hundred members, MUA has been organizing domestic workers since 1994, when it launched Manos Cariñosas (Caring Hands), a project to provide training and work opportunities for Latina home health care aides. By 2001, Caring Hands had grown to include child care workers.[7]

MUA's organizing model is representative of a key objective of the domestic workers' movement: helping its members make changes in their own lives.[8] A critical piece of MUA's work is providing leadership and community organizing trainings to "empower its members to understand the systems that oppress and exploit women, workers, and immigrants." These trainings, write Ai-jen Poo and NDWA campaign director Andrea Cristina Mercado, provide workers with the tools to "create their own vision for the world, build multi-racial alliances, and gain the tools to launch community education and organizing campaigns."[9] As members develop their skills, they may take on a greater role in the organization. This cycle presents continued opportunities for growth and development.[10]

Numerous other groups were central to organizing California's Latina, Filipina, and Asian domestic workers, including the Women's Collective of the San Francisco Day Labor Program at La Raza Centro Legal (La Colectiva), the Pilipino Workers Center (PWC), and the Coalition for Humane Immigrant Rights of Los Angeles (CHIRLA). Each group brought to the table the experiences and strategies it had cultivated through its organizing work. The organizations focused on fostering worker leadership through direct services, including establishing employment agencies that give workers power to negotiate contracts for themselves.[11]

Formed in 2001, La Colectiva is a worker-run collective that creates opportunities for economic self-sufficiency as well as personal and political empowerment through trainings and worker leadership development. The PWC, founded in Los Angeles in 1997, gives visibility to Filipina workers largely through its Caregivers Organizing for Unity, Respect, and Genuine Employment (COURAGE) Campaign, which mobilizes workers in the home health care industry. The Los Angeles–based CHIRLA focuses on multiethnic coalition building, and brought to the movement expertise in advancing the agenda for immigrant communities through advocacy, community education, and organizing. These groups shared their strategies and, working collaboratively, came together to develop a statewide campaign to improve the domestic service industry.

Maria Distancia's story shows the impact of these organizers' work. A domestic worker in California for more than ten years, the forty-three-year-old became part of the movement through

Mujeres Unidas y Activas.[12] Distancia moved to the United States at the age of twenty-one from Jalisco, Mexico, and has raised five children here. With the aid of MUA organizers, she was able to flee an abusive husband a few years ago. "I work a lot; I have been working and taking trainings from MUA and NDWA that have allowed me to get more work," she says. "I clean houses now and care for an elderly woman, and I work as a nanny for two little girls. I work more than forty hours per week every week, that's how I put food on the table for all my kids. Ever since I escaped the abuse, we're doing really well. We have problems like every family, but being outside of that situation of domestic violence has helped and supported us."

Distancia originally connected with MUA in 2005 when an organizer for the group gave a presentation about domestic violence in an English class. It was then that Distancia realized she could seek help for the abuse she was experiencing at home. She began attending MUA trainings and turned to the group's organizers for support. Distancia's experience with MUA not only helped her get out of a bad marriage; it also helped her stand up to abusive employers. "One employer would pay me with checks that would bounce," she recalls. "I stuck up for myself. I told him about the California Bill of Rights, and I told him I did this work to provide for my family. After I talked to him, the checks stopped bouncing." Distancia cites MUA's leadership trainings as having improved her ability to advocate for herself. "In the past I never would have stuck up for myself or talked to an employer directly. Now I know I can do it."

Coming Together: The 2006 California Domestic Workers' Bill of Rights

Maria Distancia was one of the many domestic workers who became part of the California Domestic Workers Coalition to advocate for the 2006 "Nanny Bill," the first piece of legislation in California that aimed to guarantee overtime pay for home child care workers. Over the course of the grassroots legislative campaign that followed, more than five hundred domestic worker leaders participated in education, outreach, and advocacy activities. Presentations and one-on-one meetings with over seventy-five community organizations helped build support for the movement; outreach focused on seniors, faith communities, and labor, women, immigrant and health and safety advocates. Hundreds of domestic workers traveled to the state capital each month to meet with legislators, lobby for the bill, and hold press conferences and rallies.

As in New York, organizers recognized that there was little or no data on the domestic workforce in California. Knowing that such data would significantly aid a legislative effort to change the existing exclusions of domestic workers from the law, MUA collaborated with the San Francisco Department of Public Health and Data Center to develop a participatory research project to evaluate conditions domestic workers faced while working in private homes.[13] (Over thirty immigrant women were trained to administer the survey, and together they conducted over 240 surveys of their peers in the San Francisco Bay Area.) Surveys were conducted in places where domestic workers were often found, including Laundromats, parks, health clinics, bus stops, and in their homes. The study found that household workers were supporting, on average, two adults and two children, but more than 80 percent were not making enough to support families of this size. One in five workers reported that in the last two months they had experienced verbal or physical abuse on the job.

Indignant at the exclusion of domestic workers from many labor laws and the rampant noncompliance with existing protections, organizers decided to start a domestic workers' rights campaign. MUA, the Women's Collective, and the Women

Workers' Project at People Organized to Win Employment Rights (POWER) formed the Bay Area Domestic Worker Rights Coalition to strategize about how to improve conditions in the industry.[14] CHIRLA and the PWC also began discussing a statewide strategy.[15] In September 2005, a meeting was held in San Francisco in which over fifty members of various domestic workers' groups participated, representing thousands of housekeepers, child care providers, and caregivers. During the two-day meeting, each organization presented its members' demands; from these, the groups culled a master list of priorities and demands. Subsequently, a delegation of domestic workers and advocates met with California assembly member Cindy Montañez to discuss what they hoped to achieve, and she agreed to introduce legislation in 2006.[16]

Montañez, thirty-two at the time, was the youngest Latina woman ever to serve in the California legislature. In her proposed domestic worker bill, AB 2536, she chose to raise two main issues: eliminating the overtime exemption for domestic workers who provide care for children, the elderly, or people with disabilities (also known as personal attendants), and instituting liquidated damages (an extra fine for employers who violate labor laws).[17] This bill provided the first major opportunity for domestic workers in California to be involved in the legislative process.

As AB 2536 moved forward in the legislature, pressure from home health agencies and disability rights advocates narrowed the scope of the bill to essentially include overtime provisions for nannies and little else.[18] The watered-down bill passed the California senate and house of representatives, but then-governor Schwarzenegger vetoed the legislation. In his veto message, Schwarzenegger emphasized the impact the legislation could have on seniors and people with disabilities:

To the Members of the California State Assembly:

I am returning Assembly Bill 2536 without my signature. This bill would require overtime pay for personal attendants who are nannies. The existing overtime exemption was intended to keep these jobs above ground and to allow those in need of such services to find assistance at a price they can afford. Removing this exemption would dramatically increase the costs of these attendants and potentially drive employment underground. I am also concerned that this bill creates new liquidated damage penalties against employers of all household workers, not merely nannies. In short, this bill subjects seniors and the severely disabled who hire household workers to a new cause for civil litigation. Given the increase in frivolous labor law litigation in recent years, I cannot support subjecting seniors and the disabled to additional liability.

Sincerely,

Arnold Schwarzenegger[19]

Schwarzenegger's veto wasn't a real surprise, given his politics on workers' rights.[20] Despite the veto, discussion of the attempted legislation raised public awareness in the state about what domestic work was and why it had economic value.

The campaign also enabled workers to tell their own stories—revealing how the intersection of class, race, nationality, and gender can shape workers' experiences.[21] One worker, María Fernández, a member of La Colectiva, pointed out:

Lack of representation makes our work invisible—a job that isn't seen has no value. . . . And that's where the differences arise, in salary, with race, for being a woman;

harassment—psychological, sexual; and even threats for any issue that comes up on the job. These factors continue to create substandard working conditions in the twenty-first century for domestic workers, with some workers still treated like the servants of old. The legislative campaigns have provided a vehicle to shed light on these abuses.[22]

Another worker, Araceli Iñiguez, added:

Attending hearings and participating in marches and protests, I began to know about laws, opportunities to participate and be part of the community. I am very satisfied to be part of it all, and now I am fighting to make my opinions heard and my rights valued, to demonstrate that I can get ahead and be a solid base as an example for my daughters' development so that they are able to study, succeed, and fight for what they want and commit themselves to their community.[23]

According to Andrea Cristina Mercado of the NDWA, the legislative process showed domestic workers "the real power and potential of a good grassroots campaign." As a result, the movement decided to put forward a second piece of legislation.[24]

The 2012 Campaign

In 2010, inspired by the campaign for a Domestic Workers' Bill of Rights in New York, as well as the growing national strength of the domestic workers' movement, the California Domestic Workers Coalition launched a second statewide campaign. With the end of Governor Schwarzenegger's term imminent and the election of a Democratic governor likely, the coalition focused on putting together a comprehensive Domestic Workers' Bill of Rights. The result of their efforts was AB 889, which was introduced in February 2011 by assembly members Tom Ammiano and V. Manuel Perez.[25]

Initially, AB 889 was used as a platform for bringing renewed visibility to domestic worker issues through the media and public discussion. In May 2011, the coalition was one of the sponsoring organizations of the San Francisco Domestic Workers Human Rights Tribunal, where workers presented compelling testimony. Juana Flores, a former domestic worker who rose to become co-director of Mujeres Unidas y Activas and a leader of the national movement as well, stated at the tribunal, "Our employers and society as a whole benefit when we are treated with dignity and respect. We need to improve our laws, from the state to the international level, in order to help ensure basic rights for domestic workers."[26]

Sustaining worker participation in the effort was not easy because of the demands of the legislative process and the fact that workers could not spend unlimited time away from their jobs and families. To adjust to this reality, coalition members organized a smaller delegation to make decisions on behalf of the larger group. Andrea Cristina Mercado noted:

> Ironically, we found the legislative process moves far too quickly to sustain democratic decision making by our memberships. Each organization named domestic worker representatives who they involved in the decision to make sure domestic workers had a voice in any policy change. This required building trust among the members in delegating decision making to staff and a few key worker leaders.[27]

As in the 2006 campaign, the coalition prioritized building relationships with other immigrant rights organizations and unions, and as a result secured widespread support from local labor unions and central labor councils. For example, Hand in Hand, an organization of employers dedicated to ensuring caring homes and just workplaces for domestic workers, became an integral part of the coalition.[28] The group brought together families who employed nannies, housecleaners, and caregivers, who supported and lobbied for the passage of AB 889. As in New York, the progressive Jewish community and other faith-based groups also played an active role in supporting economic and social justice for California's domestic workers.

AB 889 was passed by both houses of the California legislature in 2012, and the activism of domestic workers was crucial to its passage. For example, at the Assembly Labor Committee hearing on AB 889, PWC member Maria "Boots" De Chavez, a domestic worker for over ten years, described her working conditions: "You are not given the dignity you deserve. . . . [I worked] for a family that would not let me use their showers. I could only take sponge baths by the sink. . . . I have also not been allowed to use the kitchen to cook my own food."[29]

Though AB 889 was more robust than the 2006 legislation, it still was not fully representative of domestic workers' demands. For example, the initial bill would have established a standard eight-hour workday and matched the overtime protections given to other workers in California. Workers would also have gotten annual living wage increases and paid vacation and sick days. The original legislation also included overtime pay, meal and rest breaks, reporting time pay, eight hours of uninterrupted sleep for live-in household workers, and use of kitchen facilities.[30] Early versions of the bill additionally protected domestic workers from working in unsafe or unhealthy environments, and would have provided workers' compensation for those injured on the job.

The floor debate on AB 889 reflected opponents' concerns

that every provision, from overtime to meal breaks, would be too cumbersome for families of people who needed care.[31] Opposition to the bill also came from business groups. The California Chamber of Commerce came out against the legislation, which was not surprising given their position against most workers' rights legislation.[32] According to the organization, the domestic workers' bill could have created substantial wage and hour burdens that would have applied to third-party employers as well as to individual homeowners:

> As demonstrated by the overwhelming number of employment lawsuits filed on a daily basis in California, sophisticated businesses, with professional human resources staff and employment attorneys, struggle with the proper implementation of the very same onerous California-only wage and hour requirements that AB 889 seeks to impose on individual homeowners through adopted regulations, such as proper calculation of overtime wages, meal and rest periods, as well as sleep periods. AB 889 would expand this burden onto individual homeowners, who are simply seeking to hire assistance in the care for their children or elderly loved one.[33]

The chamber also argued that the legislation would deter employers from hiring domestic workers and would thus increase unemployment in California, as well as forcing homeowners and third-party employment agencies to "enter into the underground economy, as compliance with these requirements would simply be too costly."[34]

Objections to the bill were also raised by agencies like Bananas, a nonprofit child care referral and support agency founded to help families in Northern Alameda County have access to child care regardless of income. Bananas program director Judy Kriege believed that the legislation would hurt families who needed child care services. "It's a bill that really doesn't work when it comes to that kind of job," she told *Oakland North*.[35] "You can't expect a family to know what to do when they hire a nanny who comes to their home when they're at work, and then has to have breaks requiring them to leave the child." Kriege also believed that the legislation could have the unintended consequence of making it harder for nannies to find work.[36]

Groups representing the elderly and persons with disabilities were also staunch opponents of the bill. These were communities that had not been present—or at least not as vocal—during the battle for legislation in New York.[37] For example, the California Association for Health Services at Home argued that the increased regulations brought about by AB 889 could substantially burden seniors and people with disabilities. The group declared:

> While this legislation is reasonable in theory, many of the provisions are unrealistic given the realities of caring for seniors and people with disabilities in their homes. Measures such as overtime pay could nearly triple the cost of in-home care, making it unaffordable for many who wish to stay in their homes. Additionally, the bill would create a major disruption in continuity of care by requiring alternate caregivers to come into the home during sleep time, meal, and rest periods taken by the original caregiver.[38]

As a result of this multipronged opposition, on September 30, 2012, Governor Jerry Brown vetoed AB 889.[39] Brown's decision was influenced heavily by the strong resistance to the bill among advocates for people with disabilities, with the governor citing the "economic and human impact on the disabled or elderly person and their family of requiring overtime, rest and meal periods for attendants who provide 24 hour care" among his concerns about AB 889.

Deborah Doctor, a legislative advocate at Disability Rights California, said that her group wanted to support the legislation but that the question of who would ultimately pay for it was a major problem. "We're talking about balancing the needs and rights of two low-income populations," Doctor says. "Our greatest wish would be that we could support basic rights for these workers, and the only reason we're in conflict is over who pays for it. That's why we're separated on this issue." Doctor wrote a letter to the California Senate Appropriations Committee arguing against the bill in 2011. "The people with disabilities who would be affected by this bill have more in common economically with the domestic workers than they do with the wealthy whose abuse of domestic workers was the impetus for this bill," she wrote.[40] While Disability Rights California was ultimately neutral on the legislation when it came up for a vote, their early opposition clearly influenced Brown.

According to Doctor, it is hard to figure out how to make a one-size-fits-all bill when one is dealing with nonstandard working situations and relationships. "If there were a way to make this affordable for disabled people who can't pay for it, we would all be on the same page" she says. "It's hard for me to foresee how we will come to an agreement which will cost my folks money. I don't see that happening. It's applying a traditional labor model to a nontraditional working arrangement, hard to see how our concerns will be addressed."[41]

The economic struggles of the disability community are impossible to deny. Yet according to Craig Becker, general counsel for the AFL-CIO, disagreement from the disability community should not prevent establishing a floor for protections for care workers. "It is shortsighted to think we can supply this care service on the backs of workers without protections for them in place," he says. "I am sympathetic to people who need services, particularly people of limited means who are reliant on government services…. But for the long term, to think you can satisfy this need by denying basic rights to providers—it is a failure of social policy. We are going to need more care workers going forward, and the notion that the way we're going to resolve the need for increasing workers is to provide these services while at the same time keeping them outside basic protections of FLSA, seems like a recipe for failure."[42]

Despite the concerns of the disabled community, assembly member Tom Ammiano, one of the sponsors of AB 889, was nevertheless surprised by Brown's decision to reject the bill, particularly given that the questions the governor raised in his veto message (including concerns about a drafting error as well as questions about how the legislation could hurt families who hire domestic workers) could have been ironed out in the regulatory process. "We spent a lot of effort over two years—in committee hearings and through stakeholder meetings—answering many of the questions he asked in his veto message," Ammiano reflects. "We even managed to negotiate changes that swayed disability rights groups to go from hardline opponents to supporters. We thought, and we still think, we did the work to give him a bill that deserved to be signed."[43] (Governor Brown has in the past also vetoed a farm workers' bill protecting agricultural laborers;[44] these vetoes demonstrate an overall lack of support by Brown for the rights of workers in these sectors.)

Even disability rights groups were perplexed by the veto message, especially in light of the fact that Brown has cut services to the disability community.[45] With his veto message, Doctor says, "it felt like someone was trying to drive a wedge" between the disability community and domestic workers' groups.[46] According to Danielle Feris, founder of Hand in Hand and a key organizer for the 2012 California legislation, "He used the disability community's opposition as a reason, but it's conceivable that Jerry Brown vetoed the bill because of pressure from the Chamber of Commerce, and because he needed support for [other efforts like] Proposition 30."[47]

The defeat of AB 889 left many domestic workers in tears. The coalition gathered sponges and sent them to Governor Brown, telling him to "clean up his act."[48] "It was really a heartbreaking moment," Mercado says. "In the aftermath of the veto we received messages of support from across the country."

Third Time's the Charm?

Even after the 2012 defeat left organizers reeling, support from policymakers as well as the continued activism of domestic workers indicated that the movement for domestic workers' rights would continue in California. "The movement that was successful in New York was also successful in California, and the leadership was also equally strong," says Luna Ranjit, head of the New York–based immigrant rights group Adhikaar.[49]

In the continuing effort to pass a Domestic Workers' Bill of Rights, AB 241 was introduced on February 7, 2013. The legislation sought to mandate overtime, meal and rest breaks, workers' compensation, eight hours of uninterrupted sleep for live-in household workers, access to kitchen facilities, and a sanitary and separate room for live-in workers. These provisions had been identified by California domestic workers as needed improvements to their current work situations; survey research had found that 25 percent of domestic workers in California were paid less than the state's minimum wage; 91 percent did not receive overtime pay; 78 percent did not receive unpaid time off to see a doctor; and 59 percent worked when they were sick or injured. Among workers who were fired from a domestic work job, 22 percent said they were fired for calling in sick or for missing work to take care of a family member. Many also reported "extreme food insecurity."[50]

In the months following the introduction of AB 241, domestic workers lobbied heavily for the bill. For example, seventy domestic workers, along with supportive employers, traveled in vans to the state capital to lobby for the legislation as it was being voted out of the Senate Labor Committee.[51] "If I had to pick a word, it would be inspiring," recalls Mercy Albaran, communications coordinator for Mujeres Unidas y Activas.[52] "The energy was just so high. Some worker testimonies just brought the whole room to tears. These workers are so essential for our future." Like many activists in the movement, Albaran, twenty-four, is the child of an immigrant domestic worker. "My mother is a domestic worker and she suffered a lot of abuses," Albaran says. "She has worked in private homes as well as facilities. She has suffered abuse in both." Like Priscilla Gonzalez in New York, Albaran represents a second generation of immigrants who are striving to empower and establish protections for the women who raised them.

This time, the efforts of the domestic worker community paid off, as on September 26, 2013, Governor Brown signed AB 241. The workers did not win everything they wanted, such as meal and rest breaks, workers' compensation, eight hours of uninterrupted sleep for live-in household workers, and use of kitchen facilities so that workers could prepare food, but after seventy-five years of exclusion, domestic workers in California finally gained the right to overtime pay. The legislation secured overtime protection for California domestic workers who work more than nine hours per day or forty-five hours per week. The legislation includes a three-year sunset provision, requiring the state to create a committee to review the bill.[53] The sunset provision will allow the state to evaluate how the legislation is affecting people with disabilities before it can become a permanent law. Legislators who supported the bill deemed the sunset provision a necessary tradeoff to ensure the passage of a law mandating fair pay for women who earn so little.

Even though the law was pared down to little more than an overtime bill with a sunset provision, Disability Rights California still opposed the legislation for fear that it could cost people with disabilities and their families too much money[54] That the domestic worker and disability communities, both comprised of disadvantaged groups, did not feel as though they could fight together is a sign of how our economy systemically fails to see the value of domestic work and enable economic parity for vulnerable populations more generally.

Despite DRC's opposition, not all people with disabilities agree that paying domestic workers overtime would cause hardships. Nikki Brown-Booker, a person with disabilities and an employer of domestic workers in California, believes overtime requirements could actually lead people with disabilities to hire more domestic workers for shorter shifts. "My workers work long shifts and should qualify for overtime," she says. "In addition to that, long-hour shifts are not conducive to good care."[55] In Brown-Booker's opinion, there are multiple solutions to this issue that can ensure workers are paid adequately without compromising care.

Ultimately, AB 241 reflected a compromise between a growing, robust domestic workers' movement and groups who had deep concerns over the impact of the legislation, such as people with disabilities. Despite the legislative compromises, the bill is an important accomplishment for the domestic workers' movement in California and beyond.[56]

5. "Domestic Insurgents": State Campaigns and Activism in Massachusetts, Hawaii, Oregon, Illinois, and Georgia[1]

"Movements are like moving trains, they gain momentum. When it's your turn, you just hop on."—**Monique Nguyen**, executive director, MataHari: Eye of the Day

The domestic workers' movement in this country is not confined to the behemoth "blue states" of New York and California. Through organizing by workers and commitment on the part of policymakers, the movement is beginning to gain strength in other parts of the nation. New York's success has been particularly inspiring, with workers and advocates looking to the Empire State for a model as they consider how to introduce reforms in their own states. The states where domestic worker organizers have experienced some success in instigating legislation include Massachusetts, Hawaii, Oregon, Illinois, and Georgia.

Massachusetts

Natalicia Tracy is the executive director of the Brazilian Immigrant Center in Boston, as well as a PhD candidate in sociology at Boston University. In 1990, she moved from Brazil to the United States at the age of seventeen to attend college. To support herself, Tracy accepted a position as a nanny, and was told by her employer that she would be a "part of their family." In the classic bait and switch that so many domestic workers experience, Tracy's reality was far from welcoming as she found herself working eighty to ninety hours per week and living on her employer's unheated patio. She wasn't allowed to call home, couldn't receive letters, was paid twenty-five dollars per week, and did not have enough to eat. "When I look back sometimes, it is hard to believe I was able to get out of that situation," Tracy says. "I was all alone."[2]

After fulfilling her promise to work for this family for two years, Tracy found a job working for another family. This time, however, she negotiated with her new employers in advance to make sure she would have a real bedroom, as well as time to go to school. As a result of her decision to stand up for her rights, Tracy had a much more predictable work schedule and was eventually able to earn a college degree.[3] "It's like a movie sometimes when I think back to the things I had to go through," she says. "I didn't understand the rules and the laws."

As leader of the Brazilian Immigrant Center, Tracy has devoted her life to improving conditions for domestic workers in Massachusetts. The center, which was founded in 1995 and supports immigrants on issues related to workplace rights, serves workers in Boston, Cape Cod, and Bridgeport, Connecticut.[4] "We have an obligation and responsibility to change things," Tracy says. "If you start with educating the community and then change policy, you can break through this chain of abuse and discrimination." According to Tracy, the 2010 enactment of New York's Domestic Workers' Bill of Rights created the space and opportunity for activists in her state to begin their own campaign. "There are multiple reasons why this campaign is happening now," she says. "But the New York victory did inspire us in Massachusetts."

Indeed, it was Tracy's inspiring personal story that led to the introduction of the Massachusetts Domestic Workers' Bill of Rights. In 2012, Tracy met with Rep. Mike Moran (D-Brighton). Moran's mother had worked as a nanny, and Tracy's story resonated strongly with him. He agreed to introduce the Massachusetts Domestic Workers' Bill of Rights in the house, and persuaded Senator Anthony Petruccelli (D-East Boston) to introduce the bill in the senate (House Bill 1750 and Senate Bill 882, respectively).[5] "This is the stuff government should be doing," Rep. Moran said. "If we can't stick up for this segment of the population then I don't know what we're doing in government."[6]

As in New York and California, activists from several statewide immigrant, labor, and feminist groups got together, forming the Massachusetts Coalition for Domestic Workers (MCDW). MCDW is comprised of the Massachusetts Dominican Development Center, the Brazilian Women's Group, the Brazilian Immigrant Center, MataHari: Eye of the Day, and the Women's Institute for Leadership Development. A common theme among all of these groups is their focus on empowering and cultivating leadership among their members. MataHari: Eye of the Day is a ten-year-old organization in Boston that works with survivors of violence and exploitation. "I came to the organization as a volunteer and survivor of violence. I was mentored by the organization to support other survivors," says Monique Nguyen, the group's executive director.[7] MataHari does not focus on a single ethnic group, but instead offers programs with a multicultural approach. According to Nguyen, the domestic workers' movement in Massachusetts is connected to fundamental questions of workers' rights that are gaining attention—and some political traction—nationally. "Unions around the country are being dismantled. There are so many variables that have triggered the larger movement to transforming labor rights," she says.

MCDW has been able to secure support from employers of domestic workers, including several independent-living centers in Massachusetts, as well as multiple labor organizations and faith-based groups.[8] Domestic workers in Massachusetts already have the right to overtime pay—putting them far ahead of workers in New York when their campaign began. The state's pending bill of rights—which has already garnered over eighty sponsors in the Massachusetts legislature—would require one day of rest per week for domestic workers, clarity about whether a worker will be required to pay for food and lodging, privacy in worker communications, a written contract for workers who work more than sixteen hours per week, and a workplace free of harassment.[9] It would also require that all domestic workers be provided with a written description of their rights, and that the state conduct an outreach program to inform domestic workers of their rights and responsibilities.[10] The bill would additionally mandate that the state attorney general's office conduct a multilingual outreach program and make sample contracts and lists of rights available on their website.[11]

Setting Massachusetts's bill apart from those in other states, the legislation would also guarantee termination rights for live-in workers. This means that if a live-in worker is fired, he or she will receive thirty days' notice and lodging, either on site or in a comparable off-site location, *or* two weeks of severance pay. (Termination rights can be overridden by an employer's good-faith allegation of abuse, neglect, or harmful conduct on the part of the worker.) This provision may raise eyebrows, as many employees in low-wage sectors traditionally covered by labor protections have no access to severance pay—though, notably, severance is a common practice on Wall Street and in other white-collar positions.[12]

In January 2014, the domestic worker bill received a thumbs-up from the state legislature's Joint Committee on Labor and Workforce Development; as of this book's print date, the legislation was being considered by the House Committee on Ways and Means.[13] MCDW and key sponsors do not anticipate substantial opposition, and are hopeful the legislation will pass in 2014.[14]

"We are working hard, we're trying to make our case," Rep. Moran said. Speaking of the likelihood that the bill will pass in 2014, he added, "I feel good about where we are at, but I'm also not [so] naive to think it is a guarantee."

In addition to instigating the pending domestic worker bill, the movement in Massachusetts has also succeeded in establishing a mediation program for resolving disputes between domestic workers and their employers—the first in the nation. Mediation is a method of dispute resolution that is intended to foster open communication between opposing parties. Depending on the type of dispute, mediation is not always effective, particularly when the parties involved would prefer to litigate so they have a chance at winning their entire claim. In contrast to litigation, mediation involves compromise.

The main organization behind the Massachusetts program is the Brazilian Immigrant Center's Domestic Worker Law and Policy Clinic (DWLPC). The clinic, which opened its doors in 2011, specializes in responding to the unique legal concerns of domestic workers and is dedicated to representing and amplifying their voices. DWLPC also produces a manual to help educate employers and workers about their rights and obligations. The clinic's crowning achievement has been its worker-led project that trains employees and employers on how to mediate workplace disputes. Beyond its potential to resolve employment disputes, DWLPC's program illustrates another way in which the movement is helping to expand the leadership skills and abilities of domestic workers.[15] "Domestic work is a unique industry with a different kind of employer-employee relationship that is as personal as it is legal," says Lydia Edwards, director of legal services with the Brazilian Immigrant Center. "The issues are often very hurtful, personal issues related to respect and abuse and general workplace treatment inside of someone's home. It's not always cut and dry, like, 'You didn't pay me.'" Of the DWLPC's mediation program, she says, "It's an innovative, exciting project that allows for workers to be part of the problem solving for other workers, rather than relying on attorneys."[16]

Since 2011, the Brazilian Immigrant Center has litigated sixty-five cases between domestic workers and their employers.[17] About ten percent of those cases have been resolved through mediation.[18] In none of the cases that went through the mediation process did the domestic worker end up taking the employer to court. "The worker-employer relationship is so symbiotic. One doesn't exist without the other," Edwards says. "And it is a matter of keeping the process neutral, too."[19]

Not everyone is a cheerleader for using mediation as a resolution process for domestic worker-employer disputes. While Hollis Pfitsch, staff attorney with the Legal Aid Society of New York, believes that mediation can work when the employer and employee have committed to a collective bargaining process and a contract that ensures that basic standards have already been met, in her experience "with cases in which workers' rights have been violated, it is clear that many employers need litigation to give them the incentive to meaningfully engage in mediation."[20] Unfortunately, domestic workers are usually not covered by state collective bargaining laws (though they are in Massachusetts), and continue to be excluded from federal collective bargaining regulations.[21]

Ultimately, the mediation program does much more than simply resolve disputes. Including domestic workers in the process as mediators has developed their leadership and career potential.[22] "There's not always enough attorneys to go around, plus there's this untapped talent that immigrant women have," Edwards says. "Many workers have college degrees from the US or other countries that they aren't using. So we felt that here's this untapped potential and there's tons of disputes that need to be resolved."[23]

Sona Soares's experience proves this point. She earned degrees in mechanical engineering and math in Brazil before she moved to the United States at the age of twenty-two to marry and raise a child. But her husband abandoned her when her son was nineteen days old. "Becoming a domestic worker often results from a lack of options, and necessity. I had to take care of my son," Soares says.[24] She has spent three decades as a domestic worker and, after volunteering with the Brazilian Immigrant Center for many years, has become a trained mediator with DWLPC. Having worked for kind employers as well those who have treated her poorly, Soares understands first-hand the types of conflicts and conditions workers experience. "Sometimes you go home and cry a little," she says. "And the next day you get up and go to work again."

Hawaii

On April 30, 2013, just in time for May Day, Hawaii's legislature passed SB 535, the state's Domestic Workers' Bill of Rights.[25] Governor Neil Abercrombie signed the legislation in June 2013, making Hawaii the second state—after New York—to enact legal protections for domestic workers.[26] Aside from the end result, the two states' laws came about in vastly different ways. New York's legislation was the product of nearly a decade of grassroots organizing, movement building, and lobbying by domestic workers. By contrast, Hawaii's law was driven by policymakers. "Our feeling is that if six or seven states pass domestic workers' legislation like this, we can be successful at the federal level in implementing reforms to the National Labor Relations Act and other legislation that excludes domestic workers," said State Representative Roy Takumi (D-Pearl City), the key sponsor of SB 535.[27]

Takumi initially took up the cause after hearing National Domestic Workers Alliance director Ai-jen Poo speak about how domestic workers have historically been excluded from major labor protections, leaving them vulnerable to wage theft and exploitation. When Takumi introduced domestic worker legislation in Hawaii for the first time in 2011, it failed to pass.[28] In 2013, however, domestic worker legislation emerged from the Hawaii Women's Legislative Caucus, a bipartisan group that focuses on women's issues. "This bill resonated because of the women's caucus's long history of opposing all forms of discrimination, fighting for protections for women in the workplace, and the overall commitment to civil rights," State Representative Della Au Belatti (D-Makiki-Tantalus) says.[29] With this added support, as well as leadership changes in the labor, economic development, and judiciary committees, the law sailed through the Hawaii legislature with ease.

While the political saga of each state's law is very different, substantively, New York and Hawaii's bills are similar, geared toward wage protections, overtime days of rest, weekly work-hour limits, and protection from harassment and abuse on the job. Notably, neither New York's nor Hawaii's law protects domestic workers from discrimination in hiring and firing. Rep. Takumi originally drafted his bill to protect domestic workers from being terminated based on gender, race, religion, sexual orientation, or other protected classifications. However, during the hearings on the bill, religious groups in the state, including the Church State Council and the North American Religious Liberty Association, expressed concern that employers would not be allowed to fire people who worked in their homes but espoused different religious views, or attempted to indoctrinate their children with their religious views.[30]

As of mid-2014, Hawaii has seen only one wage claim filed

by a nanny. "It will take some time for people to become more aware of the law and remedies available," says Rep. Takumi. "And, unlike New York and California, the numbers of domestic workers [in Hawaii] is relatively small."[31] Hawaii is now engaged in an implementation and outreach program to make sure domestic workers are aware of their rights; the program is being led by the state's first lady, Dr. Nancie Caraway.

Oregon

Two steps forward, one step back. The same week that Hawaii became the second state in the nation to enact a domestic workers' bill of rights, similar legislation in Oregon failed. The campaign in Oregon reveals how crucial the voices of actual domestic workers are in achieving legislative victories, as well as the difficulty of getting across the message that domestic workers are doing real work that should be guided by basic protections.

The bill in Oregon was narrower in scope than its counterparts in Hawaii and New York. HB 2672, the Domestic Workers' Protection Act, would have only covered nannies, while New York's and Hawaii's laws include wage, overtime, and other protections for nannies, housekeepers, and caregivers for the elderly and disabled. HB 2672 passed the Oregon house in 2013, but ultimately died in the state senate.[32] Rep. Sara Gelser (D-Corvallis), the bill's chief sponsor, said that state senate's refusal to pass the bill was rooted in objections to providing labor protections to people who work for private families.[33] "Some legislators raised concerns about whether they'd have to still pay their nanny if she comes to Disneyland to care for the children and she is given Mickey Mouse ears," Gelser says, archly.

As in Hawaii, policymakers led the effort in Oregon. As a result, there was not much grassroots mobilization of the state's estimated ten thousand domestic workers, who are currently excluded from overtime and other protections. "I do think grassroots support can make a big difference," Gelser says. "But we also had some big, important, and competing issues this year that had been in the works longer, and our grassroots advocates appropriately focused their attention and energy there."[34] Among the activities that absorbed activists' energy was the endeavor to pass other critical legislation that could impact the families of domestic workers, including tuition equity for undocumented students who graduate from Oregon's high schools,[35] and the right to driver's licenses for undocumented people living in the state.[36] "As you can imagine, there is a lot of overlap between the advocates for all of these bills, considering they all have implications for racial equity, civil rights, and economic justice," Gelser noted.

Gelser, who was inspired to act on this issue after attending a symposium on the trafficking of women, has now made passing domestic workers' labor protections her top legislative priority. "I brought this bill late and knew it was a challenge given the many priorities that we had, and I was humbled that so many advocates were able to make time to work on this bill and to visit legislators to work on it," Gelser says. "I anticipate that now that we've raised the issue, we will be able to build even more energy behind it in coming sessions."

Illinois

In early 2013, after several years of organizing by the state's primarily Polish American domestic workers, the Illinois state senate introduced a domestic workers' bill of rights. The campaign was led by Anna Jakubek of Arise Chicago, a workers' rights organization that builds partnerships between faith and labor communities.[37] Like Natalicia Tracy of the Brazilian Immigrant Center in Boston, Jakubek worked as a nanny for several years before becoming an advocate. "My first jobs were awful. I lived in a basement room in a closet without windows and unregulated time of work," she says. "I had no breaks for holidays and instead I was working on holidays and on weekends."[38]

As was the case in New York, California, and Massachusetts, a coalition of groups in Illinois, including the Latino Union of Chicago, the Heartland Alliance, and Jobs with Justice, are backing the effort toward a domestic workers' bill. "All of this is happening in Illinois because we're seeing a growing national movement," says Jakubek, who emphasizes the need for protections by adding that domestic workers in the state face systemic challenges including practices by employment agencies that charge workers as much as a week's wages as payment for being placed in a job.[39]

To address this and other issues confronting the state's domestic workers, Illinois state senator Ira Silverstein introduced SB 1708 in February 2013.[40] The legislation seeks, among other provisions: notice and a written contract specifying wages and tasks to be performed; a minimum wage; overtime; one day off per week; advance notice of termination; eight hours of uninterrupted rest for live-in workers; and access to bathroom, laundry, and kitchen facilities.[41] Rep. Elizabeth Hernandez of Illinois's 24th District, introduced companion legislation in the Illinois House of Representatives on February 5, 2014, and Illinois workers lobbied for the legislation at the state capitol in March 2014.[42] Thus far, no major opposition to the proposed legislation has arisen.

Georgia

Georgia has held an important place in the history of domestic worker organizing ever since a group of washerwomen in Atlanta went on strike in 1881 to demand better wages and treatment.

After enduring arrests and fines, the women won their demands.[43] While decades of Jim Crow segregation and the exclusion of black workers from New Deal legislation like the Fair Labor Standards Act and the National Labor Relations Act have since weakened African American domestic workers' ability to organize, the tide may be turning, evidenced by the National Domestic Workers Alliance's activities in Georgia since 2012.

Tamieka Atkins, a lifelong organizer who was formerly with Amnesty International, is leading NDWA's Georgia chapter. Atkins has a strong commitment to organizing the state's many African American domestic workers, as well as revealing the issues that African American and immigrant communities of workers face in today's economy.[44] "The narrative of domestic work in this country is connected to slavery," Atkins says.[45] "This is the first NDWA chapter in the South, and we are deeply committed to engaging African American workers." Among Atkins's priorities is launching a job-referral program that will help members who are underemployed or unemployed find work. This program will also inform workers of the importance of employment contracts to provide clarity in expectations and avoid exploitation, and provide "know your rights" trainings so that workers understand that they cannot be denied wages. "We learned of an employer who was docking wages. If a worker showed up even a few minutes late she was denied a full hour's pay," Atkins says. "Our chapter members flagged this employer and we're in the process of developing a campaign to get them to change their policy."

The chapter is also focused on expanding Medicaid, especially after the state's governor, Nathan Deal, refused to expand Medicaid under the Affordable Care Act.[46] The Medicaid expansion would have benefited Georgia's estimated 650,000 low-income workers. The domestic workers' movement sees the issue of health care access as critical. In 2013, the chapter's progress in organizing workers across racial lines was acknowledged when Hispanics in Philanthropy, the Association of Black Foundation Executives, and the Marguerite Casey Foundation presented the NDWA with the Patiño Moore Legacy Award, which recognizes organizations that foster collaboration between Latino and African American communities.[47] Overall, Atkins and the Georgia chapter of NDWA continue to build a broad network of workers throughout Georgia to improve wages and working conditions.

It is clear that New York's model, which combined organizing with legislative advocacy, has made its mark nationally. As more states have taken up the issue of domestic workers' rights, their campaigns continue to be informed by the initial success in New York—in terms of both what can work in their state, and what cannot. As the failure of Oregon's bill makes clear, some legislators still resist the idea that basic labor protections should be extended to domestic workers. This sentiment has been mostly overcome in places where domestic workers have been central to advocacy and organizing, as the authenticity of their voices lends grassroots support to legislative efforts on their behalf. When a worker—backed by the broader movement's tenacity—arrives at a legislator's door, change becomes possible. "For this movement, the message has to come from the workers' mouths," says Lydia Edwards of the Brazilian Immigrant Center. "A legislator needs to see hear and understand directly from these workers why improved labor protections are essential."[48]

6. The Global Movement: Organizing Domestic Workers Around the World

"Although we know the US government is never interested in ratifying international standards, especially international labor standards, US activists are heavily supportive of our work."—Elizabeth Tang, International Domestic Workers Federation[1]

Born into a poor family in Brazil, Creuza Oliveira became a domestic worker at the age of ten. Unable to simultaneously maintain her work schedule and get an education, she was eventually forced to drop out of school. At work, Oliveira endured extreme abuse at the hands of employers who regularly called her "nigger," and "monkey" and beat her if she made minor mistakes. She was also sexually abused by the men in the household. And she wasn't paid a cent for her work until she turned twenty-one.[2]

In May 2012, Indian news outlets reported on the torture of a fourteen-year-old domestic worker by her software engineer employer in Noida, in the National Capital Region of Delhi. The girl was severely physically abused and forbidden from leaving her employer's home.[3]

A worker in Indonesia did not receive a single day off during her first four months on the job and, despite her strict Muslim diet, was forced to eat pork by her employers.[4]

These are just a few of the many examples of the far harsher conditions often endured by domestic workers outside of the United States as compared to the experiences of their counterparts in this country. While a lack of legal protections is common to domestic workers all over the world, domestic workers' experience in many countries outside of the United States is frequently colored by deeply entrenched sexism, racism, and classism that render the workers not just economically powerless but also vulnerable to unspeakable cruelty. Generally, there are fewer community organizers, as well as fewer resources for the community organizers who are active, in other nations than there are in the United States. This environment leaves many domestic workers—particularly those in the most patriarchal nations— with fewer advocates to turn to when they are abused.[5]

Because of this, the movement within the United States for domestic worker rights is crucial not just for protecting workers in this country, but also for making inroads abroad. Currently, leaders of the US movement are actively collaborating with partners in India, Brazil, South Africa, Indonesia, and many other countries. This work builds on the recent passage of a convention in support of domestic workers' rights by the International Labor Organization (ILO).

This chapter delves into the range of experiences of domestic workers and migrant domestic workers abroad, and how US-based activists and organizations are collaborating with the International Domestic Workers Federation (IDWF) and other global groups to address the abuses that these workers frequently experience.

"Little Better Than Slavery"

According to the ILO, domestic work comprises 7.5 percent of women's paid employment worldwide.[6] In the Middle East, one in three wage-earning women are domestic workers; in Latin America and the Caribbean, one in four female wageworkers are domestic workers. Worldwide, more than seventeen million domestic workers are children.[7] Often, the women and girls who engage in domestic work are among the least educated, come from the poorest backgrounds, and have little chance at upward social mobility.

As in the United States, domestic work globally is plagued by low wages; long hours; limited or no built-in rest time; physical, mental, and sexual abuse; and restrictions on freedom of movement. These problems are often connected to lax—or nonexistent—labor regulations, as only 10 percent of domestic workers worldwide are included within their countries' labor laws to the same extent as other workers.[8] Nearly 30 percent, or sixteen million, work in countries where they are completely excluded from national labor laws. Many other workers are partially excluded from labor protections.[9] According to the ILO, more than half of all domestic workers live in countries whose laws place no limitation on their weekly hours, and roughly 45 percent have no entitlement to weekly rest periods or paid annual leave.

While all domestic workers are vulnerable to such conditions, particularly troubling is the plight of migrant domestic workers (MDWs) who leave their home countries to work abroad. Global economic trends urge this migration, creating a deep pool of women from poorer countries who are willing to work in other nations for meager salaries, sometimes as low as one hundred dollars per month.[10] Many MDWs end up in the Middle East, as the oil boom of the 1970s prompted an influx of domestic laborers from nearby countries into that region. Approximately 1.5 million migrant domestic workers toil in Saudi Arabia; there are an estimated 200,000 in Lebanon and 660,000 in Kuwait. A large number of migrant domestic workers also toil in Bahrain, Jordan, and the United Arab Emirates.[11] Many MDWs in these countries labor in abusive situations. For example, in 2010, a twenty-three-year-old Indonesian domestic worker was tortured by her Saudi employers. The woman was brought into a hospital "look[ing] deformed as if her scalp had been peeled off.... Burns [were] scattered all over her lean body including her upper lip and fingers... She [was] bandaged all over and could hardly move or speak."[12] *The Economist* has declared domestic work in the Middle East as being "little better than slavery."[13] However, few cases of abuse are actually reported, so the true depth and pervasiveness of the problem remain largely unknown.[14]

The lack of regulation of domestic work makes possible the physical, psychological, financial, and sexual abuse of MDWs. Many countries have laws that prohibit these workers from patronizing businesses or using public facilities like beaches, rendering them essentially invisible.[15] The hiring and treatment of MDWs is also steeped in racism. For example, many Lebanese employers prefer Filipina workers because they have light skin and are believed to represent a higher class; they are therefore often more readily hired and better paid.[16] Others prefer to hire MDWs who seem "obedient." Rima Kalush of Migrant Rights, a Bahrain-based advocacy group that documents abuses of migrant workers, believes that there is "definitely a preference for migrants who are considered 'malleable' and this is sometimes attributed to particular nationalities."[17]

In addition, many employers are distrustful of their MDWs, and this leads to employment situations in which the workers are forced into confinement. According to Kalush, "There's a lot of suspicion towards domestic workers, whether it's fear that they'll steal money, harm your children, or run away.... Employers often think they're within their rights to take these 'preventative' measures, which gravely trespass on the rights of domestic workers. And they're able to do so because there's virtually nothing preventing them from doing so."[18]

Some employers fear that their workers will become pregnant, leave, or seek aid from outsiders, and thus keep them locked away. Some writers have noted that "the perceived sexuality of MDWs, especially Filipinas, is used as a pretext for employers to keep their maids locked indoors, out of fear that their maid will find a boyfriend and get pregnant."[19] This lack of trust precludes codifying actual rights for domestic workers.

Mistreatment of workers has led some countries such as Indonesia to ban their citizens from working abroad as domestic workers. (Indonesia plans to cease sending MDWs to other countries by 2017.[20]) Unfortunately, bans on migration have proven futile in terms of protecting domestic workers. In the Middle East, for example, bans have yielded higher levels of trafficking, as well as employment agencies operating on the black market.[21] These agencies render migrant women vulnerable to exploitative pay, long hours, and unconscionable contract terms.[22] Some agencies keep migrant workers in "collection" centers in the sending country for weeks or months while their country of destination processes their papers. Many of these centers are like prisons, with the women served spoiled food and not allowed to speak to one another.[23] In addition, many recruitment agents use "coercion, force, or false promises, placing women in clandestine domestic settings, illegal sex work, or exploitative sweatshops— practices that amount to trafficking."[24] Women who actually receive contracts may not be able to read them or understand that they are devoid of any protections. Often, contracts exist only between the employer and the recruitment agency, leaving the worker without any protection. According to the ILO, when employees do sign contracts with employment agencies, they may be asked essentially to sign their lives away, "agree[ing] not to seek a change of employment or employer, not to engage in 'immoral' behavior, not to marry a citizen or permanent resident, not to leave the premises of the employer without permission, and never to take a day off."[25]

MDWs also face a range of abuses connected with compensation. Even when paid on time and according to the terms of their contract, migrant workers often receive substandard wages. Employers may also charge workers rent for unlivable housing conditions, or fees for health services that they never actually receive.[26] A common practice is for employers to place payments into a bank account that they claim has been opened for the domestic worker, but to refuse her access to this account until the end of her contract. Some employment agencies give employers the option of "returning" a worker after a period of time if the worker's services are "unsatisfactory." During such trial periods, workers are rarely paid.[27]

It is clear that greater attention and regulation is critical to protecting domestic workers throughout the world. Unfortunately, the vast majority of labor laws do not include households within the ambit of "workplace." Forty percent of countries do not have any kind of regulation for domestic workers at all.[28] In many countries, domestic workers do not count as "employees" under legal definitions, or are explicitly excluded from labor codes. This essentially forces workers to be on call at all times. An ILO study in the United Arab Emirates found that not one of the domestic workers surveyed received a regular day off.[29] Against this backdrop, it is unsurprising that other protections such as maternity leave tend to be rare.[30] Globally, more than 60 percent of women domestic workers are entitled to maternity leave; however, restrictive eligibility criteria or lack of enforcement can mean that those women do not receive their benefits.[31] This poses a substantial obstacle for domestic workers who wish to balance work with their own family responsibilities.

In many countries, the idea that a domestic worker should have any legal protections is radical; this attitude is connected with the perception of domestic labor as "women's work" performed in the "private" sphere.[32] Emily Rauhala of *Time* magazine writes about how the large pool of available MDWs enables men to avoid domestic labor, "while upholding the illusion of gender equality in their own marriages...when in reality the gender inequality is simply being absorbed by less wealthy women—with all the impact that this domestic employment has on MDWs and their families back home."[33] The supply of female domestic laborers will remain high as long as domestic work continues to be thought of as "women's work," and there are no other viable economic opportunities for this population.

Push for Policy in Geneva

Juana Flores spent most of her life as a domestic worker. Born in the small town of Zacatecas, Mexico, Flores was one of eleven siblings. At the age of five, she began working in homes to earn money, caring for children and doing domestic chores. In 1981, when she was twenty-four, she came with her husband to the United States, where she worked for a Latino family, caring for their child. She was paid $150 per month. Soon, she was required to care for two other children in the family, as well as prepare the family's food and do their cleaning and washing. Despite the added responsibilities, she was not given a raise. Her employers also worked full-time, so she was essentially on duty twenty-four hours a day. Worse yet, the male head of household would regularly harass her with lewd and sexually explicit comments, and would tell her that people were going to break into the home to rape and kill her.[34]

When Flores became pregnant, her employers told her that she had to either give up the baby, or go back to Mexico. She chose to return to Mexico with her husband, where she ultimately gave birth to two children. Eventually, the family came back to the United States, settling in California. One day, when Flores was taking her children to school, another parent told her about Mujeres Unidas y Activas. When she got her next job as a care provider, Flores was aware of her rights because of her involvement with MUA. "My life changed because I knew my rights," she says.

Through involvement with the National Domestic Workers Alliance (NDWA), Flores became active in the international movement for domestic workers' rights. "I am proud. I never imagined that being a domestic worker from a young age could bring me to the movement, I never imagined I'd have this influence because of my life's work as a domestic worker," she says.

NDWA was part of a group of global organizations that in 2006 organized a conference in Amsterdam called "Respect and Rights: Protection for Domestic Workers." Over sixty representatives of domestic worker organizations, as well as trade unions, researchers, and other stakeholders, attended.[35] The discussions geared toward developing a strategy for global domestic workers' activism ultimately led to the establishment of the International Domestic Workers Network (IDWN) in 2008, which in turn evolved into the International Domestic Workers Federation (IDWF). Alongside IDWF, academics and lawyers formed the Research Network for Domestic Worker Rights to analyze domestic worker organizing and advocacy models being developed around the world.[36]

Currently, there are nearly fifty IDWF-affiliated organizations globally.[37] In 2009, soon after its founding, IDWF hired four coordinators, each working in a different region of the world: Africa, Asia, Latin America, and North America. Like NDWA, IDWF is funded through project grants from foundations, and also receives support from international trade unions, in particular the International Union of Food Workers. "Domestic workers in some countries have been included in food workers' unions, probably because domestic workers manage food preparation inside homes. So in some places domestic workers are included alongside catering workers," says Elizabeth Tang, international coordinator for IDWF.[38] The organization also receives substantial assistance from Women in Informal Employment: Globalizing and Organizing.[39] According to Tang, social networking has been crucial to IDWF's organizing efforts. "In addition to our website, we rely on Facebook a lot to connect with each other, to share news," she says. "People usually go to the website after they see something on Facebook. Twitter is less common among domestic workers and activists, though government officials use Twitter, so it is important to post there so they can see if we are really targeting them."

As a college student in Hong Kong, Tang was active in the students' rights movement, but it wasn't until she joined the Hong Kong Confederation of Trade Unions that she began to understand the importance of workers' rights.[40] Ultimately, Tang spent thirty years with the confederation, starting as a union organizer and eventually rising to CEO. "In my role at the confederation," she says, "I worked on domestic workers' issues a lot. And we were able to make a great deal of progress on the issue." Migrant domestic workers were first brought into Hong Kong in the 1970s. According to Tang, at that time there was political consensus that migrant workers should be given the same protections as other workers; otherwise employers would prefer MDWs to local workers. "It was about protecting all workers," Tang said. "The idea was, if employers do not gain anything or save money by employing migrants, they will also consider local workers. It was also about protecting local jobs."

IDWF activists set their sights on the ILO as a means of setting global labor standards for domestic workers.[41] On June 16, 2011, with many NDWA member organizations present in

Geneva, including DWU, MUA, and La Colectiva, the ILO adopted the Convention and Recommendation Concerning Decent Work for Domestic Workers, the aim of which was "protecting and improving the working and living conditions of domestic workers worldwide…and [representing] an international commitment to work on improving the living and working conditions of a very large segment of the work force which has been historically excluded, either totally or in part, from the protection of labour law."[42] Passing the convention was an arduous process. "It was not easy," says Tang, "particularly when debates were on working hours and wages, even health and safety and the role of private sectors and employment agencies—these are the most important issues to domestic workers. However, they were the most contentious, as employers and governments tried to restrict progress in these areas."

The convention was groundbreaking on an international level, for the first time moving the ILO standard-setting process into the informal economy. The convention has already had an impact globally, according to Tang, primarily because it affirmed that domestic workers are workers and cannot be excluded from protections that other workers have. "It's been almost two years since adoption of the convention," Tang said in 2013. "In Asia, it's just a bit better than the Middle East. Still, some governments have passed some protective legislation. It's still very inadequate but overall the convention was a big step in encouraging these new laws."[43]

For domestic worker activists in the United States, the passage of the ILO convention was an opportunity to have their fight for justice recognized worldwide and to see their work contribute toward improving the lives of domestic workers globally. Activists in the United States were among the most persistent and effective in influencing the passage of the ILO convention. "We are using the ILO as a tool...though the United States doesn't seem to have the political will to ratify the convention," said Luna Ranjit of Adhikaar, adding, "The United States was very active in passing the convention, but ironically the US won't ratify it." Assemblyman Keith Wright, the key champion of the domestic worker legislation in New York, sent a letter to President Obama on August 19, 2011, urging the United States to be among the first nations to ratify the convention.[44] But as with other international treaties that it has ignored, such as the UN Convention on the Elimination of All Forms of Discrimination against Women, there is no sign that the United States will ratify the convention in the near future.[45]

One important byproduct of the convention was that it cemented the relationship between American labor and the international domestic workers' rights movement. NDWA and the AFL-CIO entered into a partnership agreement before the June 2011 International Labour Conference, formalizing US labor's commitment to domestic workers' rights. According to the text of the agreement, the NDWA and the AFL-CIO together sought to strengthen "collaboration on local, statewide, national and international campaigns for recognition and labor standards for domestic workers."[46] Members of the NDWA who attended the 2011 conference were also included under the membership umbrella of the AFL-CIO, which was unusual, compared with the status of domestic workers from other nations: the majority of domestic workers present at the conference were there as observers; most were not granted membership in formal trade union organizations.[47] Among the AFL-CIO delegates was Juana Flores, who proudly told the attendees, "It has been an honor and a privilege to represent the voices of the millions of domestic workers in the United States during this process and to stand in solidarity with domestic workers across the world.... Our many years of hard work organizing among domestic workers in the United States enabled us to make a significant contribution to this process."[48]

While encouraging traditional labor unions to embrace the cause of domestic workers has had some success in the United States, this has not been the case in many other nations. For example, the Caribbean Domestic Workers Network recently called upon traditional trade unions to support its efforts to gain social security and severance benefits for domestic workers. "We find that trade unions are not lending their support to domestic workers in the region…so we are also calling on trade union leaders who say that they support the working-class people, the grassroots people…. You are hearing it but you are not seeing it," CDWN chairman Alrick Daniel said.[49]

"First, She Learned about Her Rights. Then, She Shared Her New Knowledge with Others."[50]

The ILO convention became effective in September 2013.[51] To date, twelve countries have ratified the convention: Uruguay, the Philippines, Mauritius, Bolivia,[52] Italy,[53] Germany, Paraguay, Nicaragua,[54] Tanzania,[55] Costa Rica, Guyana, and South Africa.[56] As this book went to print, Indonesia and Jamaica were close to ratifying.[57]

The convention has been a tool for mobilizing and advocacy. Since 2011, twenty-five nations have improved their legal protections for domestic workers.[58] Workers themselves are taking hold of this momentum. For example, the Hong Kong Helpers Campaign is targeting exploitative employment agencies, with workers demonstrating together, chanting, "Women united will never be divided! Migrants united will never be divided!"[59] Social media networks such as Twitter are also helping workers share information and publicize abuses.

Slowly, and in the aggregate, this activism is influencing governments around the world. Thailand passed a law protecting domestic workers in late 2012,[60] as did the Philippines.[61] Singapore passed a law providing domestic workers with weekly rest breaks. Namibia established a commis¬sion to set a new minimum wage for domestic workers and to regulate in-kind payments—a first in the country's post-independence history.[62]

Indonesia's progress since 2011 is particularly remarkable. In Elizabeth Tang's observation, one of the main obstacles to domestic worker rights in Asia and other parts of the world is that the concept of community organizing is still not as prevalent as it is in the United States. "Take Indonesia as an example. Most of the advocates, feminist organizations, are lawyers in legal organizations, some are cultural groups," Tang says. "But they are not necessarily about community organizing," she explains, or about empowering individual workers. Nevertheless, IDWF still focused on Indonesia because of the networks of domestic workers that were already established there. In addition, a draft of a domestic workers' rights bill had been submitted by the country's trade unions in collaboration with domestic worker activists. The legislation seeks wage protections, greater accountability on the part of employment agencies, and other protections. For nearly a decade, however, the legislation has sat in the Indonesian Parliament, with little hope of receiving a vote.[63]

Despite the legislative obstacles, IDWF's work in Indonesia has helped to build consensus among the country's trade unions and major domestic worker organizations—a first step to creating change. "Just consensus and establishing the cause within preeminent trade unions has taken years," Tang says. "Now, we need to get politicians to agree, otherwise the bill will continue to sit in parliament." Tang is hopeful, however. "Compared to most countries in Asia, Indonesia is unique," she says. "In other countries many labor groups do not agree with each other, and coalitions are tough. Not so in Indonesia—domestic workers were already organized. This network of domestic workers and their advocates is working really closely with us."

IDWF is also focused on India, particularly on the central state of Maharashtra, which has a more progressive government compared with those of other Indian states. Domestic workers' legislation actually exists in Maharashtra already, but it is weak.[64] "In focusing on this state we are trying to get the government to pass state-level laws in support of domestic worker protections," Tang says. "We want to build a good case in one state, show it is working, and then we can go on to the next state. That is very much the NDWA strategy in the United States." IDWF is also doing work at the national level in India, as part of a larger coalition working on labor rights. "We are also part of the national-level work, but that is our second priority," Tang says. "Our first priority is really getting something done in one state."

Worldwide, the efforts of IDWF and other global groups are already starting to pay off. Some Indian domestic workers in the city of Gurgaon, for example, successfully organized to secure health insurance benefits in 2013.[65] Domestic workers in Maharashtra have successfully organized to secure minimum wage protections.[66] Argentina adopted a new domestic worker law in 2013 that creates a maximum eight hour workday (or forty-eight hour work week), as well as offering overtime pay, a weekly rest break, vacation days, and sick and maternity leave for the nation's 1.2 million domestic workers. The law also establishes a minimum working age of sixteen for domestic workers.[67] Indonesia raised the minimum wage for domestic workers in March 2014.[68]

In Jamaica, domestic workers recently established their own union, the Jamaica Household Workers Association, which will represent the nation's estimated fifty-eight thousand domestic workers.[69] "We need to recognize that domestic workers are the ones who take care of the home affairs while their employers are involved in various aspects of national life. We could very well rename them 'ministers of home affairs,'" said Jamaican prime minister Portia Simpson-Miller. In the United Arab Emirates, policymakers are considering developing a standard contract for all domestic workers.[70] South Africa raised minimum wage protections for its domestic workers in December 2013.[71] And, as stated earlier, Singapore introduced a policy mandating one rest day per week for all domestic workers.[72]

For a myriad of reasons, it is deeply problematic to credit the United States with setting a global example for human rights.[73] That said, in the specific case of the domestic workers' movement, activists in this country—and their legislative allies—are helping to strengthen global activism and advocacy. Isolated and working in intensely patriarchal, racist, and economically stratified societies, many domestic workers throughout the world need the global movement to be robust and ambitious so that their working conditions may begin to improve. The ability of US advocates to collaborate closely with mainstream labor groups and win allies among employers and policymakers helped win the ILO convention. This progress is a testament to the women at the helm of the movement in this country—women whose devotion and work touch domestic workers abroad.

7. Collective Bargaining and Beyond: Evolving Organizing Strategies Across Low-Wage Sectors

"We've gone to thousands of doors. There's no shop floor here."—**Karen Connor**, communications director, Vermont American Federation of State, County and Municipal Employees, on organizing home care workers

"Our meetings are nothing like any labor union you can imagine. There's women of all ages, and there's always child care, food—and singing—at domestic workers' meetings."—**Premilla Nadasen**, professor, Queens College; writer and scholar on the history of domestic worker organizing.[1]

The vast majority—more than 90 percent—of domestic workers are women.[2] One-third are African American, one-fifth Hispanic, and one-fifth are immigrants.[3] Twenty-five percent are unmarried women with young children. An estimated six hundred thousand earn below-poverty wages.[4] As Jennifer Klein, professor of history at Yale University and co-author of *Caring for America: Home Health Workers in the Shadow of the Welfare State*, points out, "Home care workers are too often thought of as barriers to 'good care' for others, not a workforce facing their own barriers."[5] Klein's statement crystallizes why the domestic workers' movement is increasingly resonating with people today; namely, these workers' struggle exemplifies the economic reality so many American workers are facing. The narrative of the average American worker—and, in particular, the female American worker—has taken a troubling turn in recent years, especially with the decline of stable public-sector positions, combined with weakening labor unions.[6] In 2013, the percentage of workers who were union members was 11.3 percent, down a half percent from 2011.[7] (Women represented 72 percent of this decline.[8]) This is part of an unraveling that has spanned several decades: union membership is less than half of what it was in 1955.[9]

Concurrent with the decline in union membership has been an escalating attack on public-sector collective bargaining, which is by extension an attack on women workers. In 2011, Governor Scott Walker of Wisconsin launched a concerted effort to limit the collective bargaining rights of public employees such as teachers, nurses, child care providers, and workers in other female-dominated professions. Other states proposed similar legislation: Tennessee restricted teacher collective bargaining.[10] "In Ohio, a law repealing limits on collective bargaining was defeated in 2011.[11] And in Michigan, Governor Rick Snyder stripped the collective bargaining rights of home-based care workers in 2011.[12]

In addition to the weakening of unions, the number of public-sector jobs is decreasing, while job opportunities in the low-wage private sector—a sector with relatively limited union power—are increasing.[13] "The best we can tell, public-sector jobs have been shed recently, and women bore the brunt of that loss," said Emily Martin, vice president and general counsel of the National Women's Law Center, in an interview with *RH Reality Check*. "In the recession recovery what we have seen is loss of good unionized middle-class jobs like teaching and nursing, where women tend to dominate."[14] The women who are losing these stable union jobs are increasingly finding themselves working in low-wage, non-union positions. According to Martin, "lower-wage, service-industry positions in the private sector are seeing an increase in women employees."[15]

This trend is confirmed by Brenda Carter, communications director for Unite Here, a union that represents hotel, restaurant, textile, laundry, and other private-sector workers. In recent years, the group has seen an uptick in its female membership. "The industries that we organize are dominated by women, and anytime a new worker joins, it's likely going to be a woman," Carter says. "If two hundred workers from a hotel join our union, the largest department is usually housekeeping—which is almost always all women."[16] In the absence of strong unions, Emily Martin believes, "antidiscrimination laws, family medical leave, wage and hour protections need to be stronger and aggressively enforced so there are baseline protections for all workers." However, many of these protections, particularly paid leave, are not available to most workers.

Domestic Workers and State Collective Bargaining Laws

Despite the hostile climate toward unions and collective bargaining—and by extension toward women workers—public-sector home care workers (that is, domestic workers who are paid by Medicaid, Medicare, or other pools of public money) have managed to secure collective bargaining rights in several states. Even though these workers are paid out of public funds, they are often independent contractors with no benefits. The insecurity of these jobs compelled publicly paid home care workers to begin unionization campaigns in the 1970s and 1980s, about a decade before awareness around privately employed domestic workers began to increase. As a result of their early activism, Eileen Boris and Jennifer Klein write in *Dissent*, "tens of thousands of home care workers began to win some of the standard features of employment most Americans take for granted: a regular paycheck, workers' compensation, and grievance procedures."[17]

Their first major success was in California, where in 1992

the Service Employees International Union collaborated with consumer advocacy groups to win legislation that established a legal employment relationship between home care workers and the state for the purpose of collective bargaining.[18] David Rolf, a home care worker organizer in Los Angeles, told the *New York Times* in 1999 that the effort "reached out to low-income, women workers, workers of color, and immigrant workers. If you look at the demographic changes in Southern California, the labor movement has to figure out how to bring these workers in because they are the backbone of the new, low-wage service-sector economy."[19]

These collective bargaining laws are credited with helping to reduce the poverty rate, as well as improving the retention rate of California's publicly paid home care workers.[20] Candace Howes, a professor of economics at Connecticut College, evaluated the economic impact of increasing these workers' wages, finding that raising wages for home care workers in San Francisco County reduced the county's overall poverty rate by 16 percent.[21] In addition, as wages increased, the retention rate of home care workers in San Francisco rose by 9 percent and the retention rate for new home care workers rose by 89 percent.[22]

Since California first showed the way, Oregon, Washington, Illinois, Massachusetts, and Missouri have also codified collective bargaining rights for their publicly paid home care workers.[23] (None of the state laws allow workers to strike; this exclusion is so that recipients of care continue receiving vital services without interruption.)[24] In May 2013, Vermont became the latest state to establish collective bargaining rights for home care workers.[25] Janelle Blake, who has been a home care worker in the state for more than ten years, supports the new collective bargaining legislation. "I don't even know my colleagues," she says. "We are all spread out in the state of Vermont; we don't know each other.

And that's why it's so great to form a union. When we come together we can get more done." [26] For the purposes of collective bargaining, Vermont's law will make Blake and other home care workers state employees.

Blake earns $9.78 per hour as part of Vermont's Medicaid-funded home care program. She works a total of sixty-eight hours per week—full time caring for a woman with disabilities, and part time caring for a young boy with disabilities. Early in her career, Blake was a home care provider for a man with Alzheimer's; she also worked as a special education teacher. Blake, along with her convenience store manager husband, has also raised her own three children, all while working in the care sector. "It almost came to the point of losing our condo because things were getting so expensive," she says. "It got really scary; that's why I'm working so hard. We've worked very hard for everything we have; we started on food stamps and came up from there."[27]

Recent research is consistent with Blake's experience. The Great Recession, Klein and Boris write, has been a "triple whammy" for home care workers:

> The housing and mortgage crisis threatened their very workplace—their homes or the homes of those they cared for; the fiscal crisis of the state led to cuts in funds that paid their wages through long-term care programs; and the conservative political backlash and Republican ascent of 2010 opened an assault on their hard-won collective bargaining rights, wage increases, and recognition as "workers."[28]

Attack in the Federal Courts: Harris v. Quinn

Despite the handful of successes they have achieved over the years, domestic workers are still not included within collective bargaining statutes in many states, or at the federal level. This leaves most women like Janelle Blake who labor in the care sector excluded from any type of collective bargaining structure.[29] And the US Supreme Court may significantly restrict the collective bargaining rights of these home care workers and all publicly paid employees. In the case of *Harris v. Quinn*, which is currently before the Supreme Court, "right-to-work" forces are pushing the state of Illinois to dismantle the collective bargaining rights of its state employees, including home care workers.[30] The plaintiff in the case—a home care worker who is represented by the National Right to Work Legal Defense Foundation—argues that the mandatory union fee assessed by the state violates her First Amendment rights. While the Seventh Circuit Court of Appeals resoundingly dismissed this argument in 2011, holding that states have clear authority to assess union fees, it is unclear how the Supreme Court will treat this issue.[31]

In an amicus brief filed on behalf of the state of Illinois, Eileen Boris and Jennifer Klein write, "Many homecare workers in America are at the vulnerable intersection of racial, gender, and socioeconomic disadvantage. On the whole, these workers are disproportionately women of color."[32] Of the home care workers who would be affected by a repeal of collective bargaining statutes in Illinois, the majority are women, 50 percent are African American, and 25 percent are Hispanic.[33] In addition to arguing that repealing collective bargaining rights would disproportionately affect economically disadvantaged populations, Boris and Klein's amicus brief also shreds the argument that home care work is frequently voluntary and therefore should not be included within collective bargaining protections:

> This history of homecare's increasing development as a distinct occupation—and the consistent recognition

of state governments that they are responsible for the continued availability of quality homecare—belies the assumption that seems to underlie much of petitioners' argument: that many homecare providers are best characterized as volunteers "caring for a disabled family member so that he or she may live at home"…rather than as members of a critically important and sophisticated government workforce.

The American Federation of State, County and Municipal Employees (AFSCME) has also brought attention to the gender and economic implications of the case. In the *Huffington Post*, the union's secretary-treasurer, Laura Reyes, wrote:

Let's be candid about why cases like *Harris v. Quinn* are rising to the Supreme Court. Women make up 45 percent of union membership and will become the majority by 2020. That has anti-worker forces worried. They know that if women enjoy collective bargaining rights and have a strong voice in their workplaces, the inequalities of the past—which favored their power and bottom line—will begin to fade away. Nearly 60 percent of women would earn more if they were paid the same as men, and the poverty rate for women would be cut in half. [34]

The fact that the plaintiff in *Harris v. Quinn* is a home care worker speaks volumes about the tactics taken by the conservative "right-to-work" movement, which has latched on to women-dominated public positions in its efforts to destroy public-sector unions. That the symbol of their activism is a home care worker is indicative of their view that engaging in domestic work is a "voluntary" choice driven solely by the worker and not her context and circumstances; that it is motivated by compassion and is thus not "real" work.

Non-Traditional, Non-Union Organizing Forces

Harris v. Quinn notwithstanding, there is debate within the domestic workers' movement about whether collective bargaining is the right strategy in today's economy. This debate is illustrated by what happened in New York when, after passage of the Domestic Workers' Bill of Rights in 2010, the New York State Department of Labor was directed to conduct a study examining whether collective bargaining was feasible for domestic workers under the State Employment Relations Act (SERA). The statute protects workers' rights to collectively bargain and prohibits employers from interfering with unionization, monitoring workers who organize together, or blacklisting organizers. SERA applies primarily to private-sector workers who are not covered by the National Labor Relations Act, such as employees of small companies. As with the NLRA, domestic and farm workers are not covered.[35]

The Department of Labor study highlighted a number of challenges domestic workers could face in attempting to bargain collectively, notably that they are decentralized within communities, and that employers often hire only a single worker.[36] The study also pointed out that collective bargaining would require a significant paradigm shift in how employers view their domestic workers, as many employers may be uncomfortable treating their domestic workers as employees or discussing employment terms and conditions with them. In addition, the study stated, "There are also likely to be greater emotional attachments arising within domestic labor relations than may be typical in an industrial or service context."[37] In response to the study, DWU, NDWA, and other groups published their own report advocating for immediate inclusion of domestic workers under SERA.[38]

Even though movement activists have sought inclusion within New York State's collective bargaining statute, there has also been hesitation about whether expending resources and political capital in this area is necessarily the best strategy for domestic workers. "The reality is that the traditional model of collective bargaining under the National Labor Relations Act framework doesn't quite fit for our workforce," Ai-jen Poo of the NDWA told *In These Times*. "Even if we weren't excluded from the NLRA, there's no collective, and there's no one to bargain with—none of the traditional kinds of assumptions are there."[39]

If anything, exclusion from the NLRA, state collective bargaining legislation, and other labor protections, along with the reality of low wages and economic insecurity, has forced greater activism by domestic workers and other non-union groups.[40] In a 2013 essay for *Dissent*, Josh Eidelson wrote about organizing by guest workers who come into the United States for brief periods of time and often labor under harsh working conditions. Eidelson reported that workers at CJ's Seafood in Louisiana were subject to surveillance by management inside and outside of work, were sometimes required to be on the job twenty-four hours per day, and were threatened if they tried to leave. In 2011, eight CJ's workers went on strike to protest their conditions. Eidelson writes, "The CJ's workers settled on a plan to approach their boss as a group with a list of modest demands: providing a full lunch break, turning off some of the cameras, and firing the supervisor who kept threatening to beat them with shovels."[41] While the eight strikers did not ultimately secure collective bargaining rights or shut down their workplace, they did gain national media attention and build public support for reforms. "In other words," Eidelson wrote, "they used the kinds of comprehensive campaign tactics that have increasingly come to typify successful labor struggles in the United States: a blend of workplace activism and media, consumer, legal, and political pressure." With the decline of traditional unions and the swell of low-wage job opportunities, the strike at CJ's shows how workers are, by grave necessity, generating new models for organizing.

One non-union group that is embracing these new organizing models is Restaurant Opportunities Centers United (ROC), which has been active in securing paid sick days for its members as well as in raising awareness about the particular stresses women in the restaurant industry face in securing care for their families.[42] ROC is what is known as a worker center—a nonprofit that organizes low-wage workers who are not part of a union or some other collective bargaining group. The number of these centers has increased dramatically over the past several years. Today, there are more than two hundred worker centers in the United States, representing workers in the restaurant, retail, and construction industries.[43] Based in New York and Oakland, ROC is led by Saru Jayaraman, who believes that "collective bargaining is not always the best model for everyone. We are not engaged in collective bargaining; we are organizing multiple stakeholders."[44] Like NDWA, ROC has also found success by organizing employers to become advocates for the rights of the workers.

The Chinese Progressive Association (CPA) is a non-union group that has been organizing San Francisco's Chinese community since 1972. In 2001, the group started a worker-organizing center to address issues faced by Chinese immigrant restaurant and domestic workers. According to CPA's executive director, Alex Tom, the decline of San Francisco's garment industry forced many of the women CPA serves into lower-wage sectors including care and restaurant work. "They are basically doing jobs that are highly underemployed. Even if they're a home care worker, they may only get five to ten hours per week," he says. "And patriarchy cuts into this, too. Chinese immigrant women are expected to provide child care for their own children at the same time. So sometimes they're not able to find full employment."[45]

CPA has a job-training program that aims to help Chinese immigrant women find stable employment. "It's a complex web of issues," Tom says. "Women in the Chinese immigrant community take the brunt of everything. Immigrant men that come to this country are used to being the breadwinner in China, or their home country, and face a lot of pressure when they get here, so they feel challenged when their wives earn. Chinese immigrant men take out the exploitation they experience in the workforce on their family. It is about wage exploitation, how capitalism is rearing its ugliest impacts on society right now."

CPA too has pursued local and state initiatives to help secure labor protections for its membership. For example, the group worked to secure San Francisco's paid sick leave and minimum wage ordinance, which passed in 2006.[46] CPA was also a supporter of the California domestic workers' legislation. "A domestic workers' bill of rights will be a huge advance for all people including people in the Chinese community," Tom said in the months before the bill was passed. "Lots of single elder Chinese women work as nannies."

Another success story involving a non-union workers' organization is that of the Fair Food Program in Florida. The program is a collaboration between the Fair Food Standards Council (FFSC) and the state's tomato farmers devoted to helping enforce the Fair Food Code of Conduct, which prohibits discrimination, sexual abuse, and harassment, among other provisions. Ten professional FFSC) monitors conduct announced and unannounced audits of the state's tomato farms, which involve intensive worker interviews. "We assess whether a company has systems in place that can comply with the Fair Food Code of Conduct and then whether in fact they're being implemented at field level," says

Laura Safer Espinoza, a former New York State Supreme Court judge who is now director of the Fair Food Standards Council. "If violations are found, growers are given an opportunity to correct them through a corrective action plan. If they fail to do so, they can be suspended from the program."[47]

The program applies to both women and men agricultural workers, but in terms of preventing sexual harassment, it primarily benefits women. (Female tomato farm workers have long faced endemic sexual harassment at the hands of their supervisors.)[48] By 2010, 90 percent of all Florida tomato growers and buyers had signed on to the program; any tomato grower who fails to abide by the code of conduct is barred from selling in the state. "There is a powerful market consequence that gives this program teeth," says Judge Espinoza. "It is a privilege to be involved in a program that goes beyond the legal system in terms of its capacity for transformational change." The program may be replicated in other states and among growers of other types of agricultural crops. Women farm workers have deepened their organizing overall, as evidenced by the formation of the Alianza Nacional de Campesinas (National Alliance of Farmworker Women).[49]

There are signs that these new types of organizing models are influencing business leaders to make changes to wage and benefits practices without the mandate of local or national policy. Zingerman's Community of Businesses is a group of eight food-based businesses, including a restaurant called Zingerman's Roadhouse, all located in the Ann Arbor, Michigan, vicinity. With one of its guiding principles being "to enrich as many lives as we possibly can," Zingerman's offers all of its employees—part-time and full-time—health and dental benefits, and paid time off. After they have worked at Zingerman's for one year, employees are eligible for the company's 401(k) program.

In 2013, Zingerman's began cultivating another dimension

to its employee-centered business: the concept of a "thrive-able wage." The company composed a vision statement on this concept, stating, "We [are raising] wages to a 'thrive-able' level throughout the organization and there is a powerful multiplier effect going on. Higher wages lead to higher morale and are the engine that keeps everything spiraling upward. In many cases, productivity increases due to lowered stress levels in the lives of the people in our organization because of assurance that their financial needs are covered."[50] Moving to a "thrive-able wage" reflects an understanding that employers are part of a larger ecosystem of workers, their families, and their communities and should not just bow to partners and shareholders. "Just as an ideal democracy does the work of teaching everyone how to vote responsibly," the company wrote in the vision statement, "we as a business give to all our members an understanding of finance as a fundamental tool."[51]

Workers' Rights and Online Platforms

Enhanced infrastructure, especially web-based communication, plays an important part in allowing nascent worker alliances to organize more easily and effectively. Indeed, advocates like Rocio Avila in California have noted that online resources have enabled domestic workers to connect with advocates and community organizers.[52]

Some workers' rights activists have begun to focus specifically on enhancing online infrastructure that can benefit all labor organizing. Since 2012, a fledgling online platform called Coworker.org has emerged to aid workers who are seeking to change their employers' policies.[53] In contrast to Facebook and other online platforms that can aid organizing, Coworker.org is devoted exclusively to organizing workers. The founders of Coworker.org, Jess Kutch and Michelle Miller, are former union organizers and former staffers of Change.org, a free online petition platform that it utilized for many social justice causes.

"We realized there weren't spaces online for workers to learn from each other. Imagine if there's a place online where you can see every active paid maternity leave campaign in the country," Kutch says. "We're in the very early stages of this, but as we get to scale we're going to have awesome opportunities to connect dots for people and to link them to experienced workplace activists. This is not just about workers influencing their employers; it's also about being able to see what other groups of workers are doing."[54]

The employees of the Juicy Couture retail chain were among the first groups to create a campaign using Coworker.org. In 2013, the management of Juicy Couture was accused by former employees of cutting its workers' hours in order to avoid implementing the Affordable Care Act (ACA).[55] This made Juicy Couture the latest employer accused of contributing to the "part-timeification" trend now popular in the restaurant, retail, and other sectors. After the ACA became law, some employers began cutting worker hours so as to save money and avoid the requirements of the health-care reform law. The *New York Times* reported in 2012 about the "part-time lives" of an increasing number of employees.[56] "Over the past two decades, many major retailers went from a quotient of 70 to 80 percent full-time to at least 70 percent part-time across the [retail] industry," Burt P. Flickinger III, managing director of the Strategic Resource Group, a retail consulting firm, told the *Times*.[57]

This is a trend that disproportionately affects women, since women are more likely than men to work in part time positions.[58] The Retail Action Project, which is partnering with Coworker.org on the Juicy Couture campaign, points this out in their advocacy materials: "As retail businesses around the country institute around-the-clock holiday sale hours, it is women who are working extra, for less pay and benefits than their male counterparts."[59]

Ali, a twenty-two-year-old college student, worked at Juicy Couture's flagship location in Manhattan.[60] She was hired during the 2012 holiday season to work thirty to thirty-five hours per week. After New Years Day, Ali says her hours were cut in half with little advance notice. Ali, whose last name is being withheld for reasons of privacy, complained about the loss in hours, and she was fired in 2013, ostensibly for tardiness. "Being late was a legitimate reason to fire me, but it's also possible they fired me because I was outspoken about the hours issue," she says. "I spoke with every manager in the store about it."[61] (A representative for Juicy Couture said, "While we do not share specific details about our associates, we would not fire an employee for speaking their mind.")[62]

Coworker.org offers workers like Ali guidance—for example, encouraging them to avoid creating petitions at work, or on work computers, to avoid retaliation. "Without organizers behind the scenes figuring out ways to grow those communities and win battles over time, you're just going to have disparate communities never building toward something," says Kutch, adding that she and Miller hope to engage a network of workers' rights attorneys to assist employees who are facing retaliation for their organizing activities.

Tools like Coworker.org may become more important for workers' rights advocacy across sectors, as workers continue organizing outside of the collective bargaining context. While online tools may not be as easy for many domestic workers to access given socioeconomic barriers as well as isolated working conditions, such tools can supplement community organizing efforts that are already in place.

The Model Alliance

Similar to domestic workers, other groups of workers have begun to appeal to state legislatures to improve labor protections in their sector. One group that has begun to have success is the Model Alliance, a nonprofit organization that advocates for better working conditions for children and adults in the fashion industry.

Fashion models are not generally perceived as "workers" in the way most labor rights advocates understand the term. However, the most successful, elite fashion models are really the proverbial "1 percent," as Sara Ziff, a model of fifteen years and founder of the Model Alliance, calls them. Ziff has taken it upon herself to educate both labor rights activists and the fashion industry about why working conditions for models need to improve. "Modeling seems like a privileged profession, so the general public attitude is not at all sympathetic [to organizing efforts]," she says. "Most people have a hard time even understanding that it is work."[63]

Most models are independent contractors and are thus unprotected by major labor laws and vulnerable to retaliation by employers if they choose to organize. According to Ziff, many members of the Model Alliance join anonymously, so that their chances of getting work aren't diminished. While actors can join the Screen Actors Guild once they have fulfilled a certain amount of acting work, there is no such union for models.[64]

Even though modeling is one of the few sectors in which women earn more money than men, the majority of women and girls trying to work as models have a difficult time making a buck. Their earnings are shoveled to agents (many models end up in debt to their agencies) while they are expected to pay for their own lodging and transportation.[65] Paying off their debts is sometimes impossible as designers often pay models with clothes and other products instead of with a paycheck—in 2012 designer Marc Jacobs faced criticism for this, though he has since changed this practice.[66] The average model's salary in 2011 was $33,000 per year, but there is wide variance in salary as some models make up to $400,000 per year while others are swimming in debt.[67]

Like domestic workers, models are rarely paid overtime, no matter how late into the night they may work on a shoot.

The Model Alliance also seeks to end sexual harassment and assault in the fashion industry—which some contend is widely underreported by models fearful of losing work—as well as questioning basic standards of beauty that promote unhealthy images of women, and improve protections for minors working as models. "You see fourteen- or fifteen-year-old girls coming to New York to model, and these kids are not thinking about their rights," Ziff says. "They might even feel lucky to have a picture in a magazine and not ask if they're getting paid."

Thousands of girls and young women flock to New York City each year to pursue their dreams, but the city's labor code for years did not include protections for child models. Even though New York has been a leader in some of the most cutting-edge labor movements, the city neglected its child models, lagging behind more than twenty states, including Alabama, Missouri, North Carolina, and Texas, that do protect child models in their labor codes.[68] And these children need protection: a white paper released in 2013 by the New York Senate Independent Democratic Conference found:

> Approximately 30% of female print and runway models have experienced inappropriate touching while modeling. Another 28% experienced pressure to engage in sexual intercourse at the workplace during their career. Greater than three-quarters of models (77%) admitted to being exposed to alcohol and drugs while working. These numbers are extremely alarming. This is only amplified when one considers that a mere 29% of models experiencing some form of abuse were comfortable with reporting it to the agency representing them.[69]

The Model Alliance began educating state policymakers about this issue, and Senators Jeffrey Klein (D-Bronx) and Diane Savino (D-Staten Island) introduced legislation to protect child models in the state. According to Anna Durrett, a spokesperson for the two legislators, there wasn't any awareness around this issue until the Model Alliance came along. "It was just a question of organizing," Durrett says. "There wasn't anyone like the Model Alliance around to galvanize people around this."[70]

In September 2013, Ziff testified at the New York State Department of Labor about working conditions for child models as well as their exclusion from labor protections. She also wrote an editorial about the issue for the *New York Times* and created a petition asking Governor Andrew Cuomo to take action.[71] After the Model Alliance placed a spotlight on the working conditions of child models, as well as the policy exclusion, Senator Klein reached out to Ziff and began working on child model protections. "It wasn't without effort, but [the legislators] really came to us," Ziff says.

As a result, in October 2013, New York enacted its first-ever child model law, adding "print and runway models" to the list of child performers protected by Department of Labor regulations. The legislation requires designers who hire print and runway models under the age of eighteen to put a portion of the model's earnings into a trust. The law also requires designers to hire chaperones and tutors for young models on shoots.[72] BuzzFeed's Amy Odell pointed out soon after the legislature's vote that "the law is expected to affect female models more than male models, who tend to start their careers a little older."[73]

In the wake of its legislative success, the Model Alliance is collaborating with Fordham Law School and the Fashion Law Institute; it now plans to focus on ending payment-in-trade practices and changing a host of other troubling working conditions. "Modeling can be wonderful work," Ziff says. "But hearing other models' stories has made clear that bad experiences in the business—lack of financial security, sexual harassment—are systemic and need to change."

In her thoughtful essay "An Imminent Hanging," Washington University law professor Marion Crain notes that the weakening of the National Labor Relations Act is forcing workers to find new ways of organizing.[74] Crain writes, "The possibilities for [reforming the National Labor Relations Act] are politically charged, and some seem paramount to rearranging deck chairs on the Titanic." She quotes a West Virginia coal miner who, while on strike, said, "We have plenty of law, but not enough justice." Recent employment rights–related decisions by the Supreme Court, in particular, seem to buttress this worker's sentiment.[75] The Court could further roll back collective bargaining in *Harris v. Quinn*.

As in the domestic workers' movement, workers across many sectors, from farm and retail to restaurant and fashion, are advocating for themselves in the face of grave economic conditions, winning results without relying on New Deal–era frameworks. Despite the continued backlash against collective bargaining, the current labor landscape reveals diverse strategies around which workers can mobilize and make change through appealing to policymakers as well as the public at large.

8. Valuing Care Means Valuing Parents

"There are people on disability who are caregivers themselves. There are so many nuances to this, it's not a simple dichotomy of people who need care and give care. There's a whole area in between."—**Sarita Gupta**, executive director, Jobs with Justice, co-director, Caring across Generations

One of the sad ironies of care work is that many domestic workers struggle to afford care for their own families. A range of policies—or more accurately, an absence of supportive policies—in the United States make it difficult for many middle- and lower-income people to obtain care for their loved ones while they are working. Most workers in the United States have no access to paid family leave—a gap that crystallizes the way domestic labor is viewed, as a practice devoid of economic value. Rather than viewing people who leave the workforce for the private sphere as sustaining their productivity by raising a child or caring for a family member, our economy generally cuts caregivers out of the equation entirely. In her edited volume *For Love and Money: Care Provision in the United States*, economist Nancy Folbre of the University of Massachusetts Amherst points out that so much care work takes place on an unpaid basis that it drives down wages for those who do get paid for it, contributing to a cyclical pattern in which care work is not treated as part of the larger economy.[1]

But this economic reality does not jibe with the actual demand for care. The total number of Americans in need of long-term care is expected to rise to twenty-seven million by 2050.[2]

The most significant factor increasing this demand will be the growth of the elderly population (people over the age of sixty-five), which is expected to more than double from forty million currently to nearly ninety million by 2050.[3] (It is also projected that personal and home-care aide jobs will increase 50 percent by 2018.[4])

Folbre also makes a strong argument about the public benefit of care work, which she believes should be factored into how wages are allocated and labor is valued generally. She writes, "The public benefits of successful care are particularly large relative to the private costs because care work contributes to the development of human capabilities that influence the quality of virtually all social transactions."[5] Tying compensation to public benefit rather than to skill would yield higher wages for domestic workers.

One of the purposes of Caring across Generations, a joint campaign by NDWA, Jobs with Justice, and other groups, is to address the interconnected needs of domestic employers and workers. The goal of the organization is to make inroads in five key areas: training for workers who care for the disabled and elderly; affordability of care for the disabled and elderly; a path to legal status and citizenship for immigrant workers; job quality; and job creation.[6] "We should be fighting for dignity for the aging population, for people with disabilities, and for workers," says Sarita Gupta, co-director of Caring across Generations. "We can win dignity all the way around."[7]

A policy shift that would help many lower- and middle-income families would be broadening access to paid family leave. While the Family Medical Leave Act has been on the books since 1993, it guarantees only up to twelve weeks of unpaid leave—a completely unrealistic amount of time for most people with ailing family members or children to be without income. In recent years, policymakers across the country have begun to throw their weight behind paid family leave laws. The New York State Assembly voted in March 2014 in favor of paid family leave, offering workers paid time off to care for an infant or ill relative.[8] If the bill is signed into law, New York will become the fourth state to offer paid family leave, after California, New Jersey, and Rhode Island.

The New York State Legislature's vote on paid family leave came days after the New York City Council expanded access to paid sick days.[9] New York City thus joined San Francisco, Washington, DC, Portland, Seattle, and Philadelphia as one of the only cities in the nation with paid sick leave ordinances.[10] (Connecticut is the only state currently with a paid sick leave ordinance, though campaigns for similar policies exist in at least eight states.) In response to the New York City Council's vote, Debra Ness, president of the National Partnership for Women and Families, an organization that promotes fairness in the workplace and health care rights, released a statement noting that the vote "to strengthen the city's already historic paid sick days law is a testament to lawmakers' strong commitment to workers, families, public health and businesses in the city."[11]

The National Partnership is currently working with Representative Rosa DeLauro of Connecticut on a bill that would extend paid family leave to all Americans.[12] Part of the rationale behind this push for paid leave is new survey data showing increased interest among members of Congress in addressing women's issues, particularly after the 2012 elections in which the women's vote was instrumental.[13] Despite the interest from policymakers, the fight for a national paid family leave program is still going to be a long one. "We're under no illusion this will pass easily," Vicki Shabo, director of Work and Family Programs at the National Partnership of Women and Families, said in 2013.

"But we're building momentum in Congress and assembling a broad coalition around the country, similar to the one that was behind the Family Medical Leave Act of 1993."[14]

The California Paid Family Leave (PFL) program, which began in 2002, has demonstrated how paid leave can help low-income families. A report by the University of California, Santa Barbara, evaluated the effects of the PFL program on families' economic security, stating:

> Leave under the PFL program had the biggest impact among workers that researchers categorized as employed in "low-quality" jobs or jobs that did not pay at least $20/hour with health insurance. Among these workers, 91% of them who used the PFL program for their leave reported that their leave improved their ability to care for a new child, compared with 71% of workers who did not use the PFL program. Seventy-two percent of workers in "low-quality" jobs who used the PFL program reported that it improved their ability to arrange child care compared to 49% of workers who did not use the program.[15]

The study also found that paid family leave enabled women to increase their working hours after returning from leave, "with a concomitant increase in earnings."

As mentioned, currently, only two states besides California have paid family leave programs: New Jersey and Rhode Island.[16] (Washington passed a program in 2007, but it has been indefinitely postponed by the state legislature because of a lack of funding.[17]) New Jersey's program, enacted in 2008, provides short-term paid leave for employees who need to care for an ill spouse, parent, or child, or who have a new child. The program is financed by state employees, who can elect to contribute one-tenth of 1 percent of their salary in exchange for up to six weeks of paid time off from work.[18] From July 2009 through April 2013, $281.2 million was paid out for nearly one hundred thousand claims, most of which was for parents with infants.[19] New Jersey employees have actually used less sick time than the program allows.

Despite advances in states like New Jersey, most workers in the United States do not have access to paid family leave. And, as is true for most benefits, employers are under no obligation to offer paid leave. And far fewer men than women have parental leave, in part because corporate and public policy and culture still tells fathers that their place is in the office.[20] According to the *Wall Street Journal*, 85 percent of US firms do not offer any paid leave for men.[21] By contrast, 50 percent of businesses offer paid maternity leave. This policy disparity neglects the critical role fathers play in families and their children's lives. While some larger firms have begun to alter their policies—Yahoo! president and CEO Marissa Mayer recently doubled her employees' paternity and maternity leave—overall, support for dads' time with their children remains sparse.[22]

"We think it's great that some companies are offering paid leave and benefits to new fathers as a means of attracting and retaining talent, but we are also mindful that that is the exception and not the rule," says Vicki Shabo. "Most new fathers don't have paid leave when their children are born."[23]

Good for Business, Bad for Families

A tenet of capitalism is that companies should limit or decrease costs as much as possible for the purpose of increasing profit. In line with this value, employers have no legal obligation to offer paid leave, health care, 401(k) plans, or other benefits.. While local and national policies can help change this to some degree, support from the private sector is critical. However, what many companies fail to realize is that the lack of pro-family policies hurts both workers and business over the long run. The belief that a conflict exists between employers' commitment to profit and pro-family policies was strikingly illustrated in February 2014 when Tim Armstrong, chairman and CEO of AOL, said the following about cuts to the company's 401(k) plan during a staff conference call:

> We had two AOL-ers that had distressed babies that were born that we paid a million dollars each to make sure those babies were OK in general. And those are the things that add up into our benefits cost. So when we had the final decision about what benefits to cut because of the increased healthcare costs, we made the decision, and I made the decision, to basically change the 401(k) plan.[24]

While Armstrong's comments were not directly related to family leave, his statement reveals the tension employers perceive between the pursuit of profit and commitment to employer-supported family policies. Armstrong was speaking about the cost of health care for workers facing serious medical issues—and specifically, the fact that these costs reduce company profits, never mind that his workers had paid their health care premiums so that they'd be covered in such health emergencies. Armstrong also held this view despite the fact that his company is immensely profitable, with revenues of $2.3 billion in 2013.[25] (Armstrong restored the company's previous 401(k) benefits and publicly apologized following public outrage about his comments.[26])

In terms of having a pro-family environment, AOL has been listed among the one hundred best companies for working mothers, for offering "lactation rooms, backup dependent care and expansive parenting programs and leaves."[27] Armstrong's remarks notwithstanding, AOL is not generally considered a bad employer. Yet his comments reveal resistance to pro-family policy, despite the fact that such policy has been shown to have a positive impact on business. According to a policy brief by Cassandra Engeman, a Ph.D. candidate in sociology at the University of California, Santa Barbara, "[f]amily leave programs, in general, benefit businesses, and the pay-off for providing leave may exceed the cost of not providing it."[28]

There are private-sector employers who are committed to pro-family policies, to varying degrees. Clothing designer and "perennially profitable" retailer Eileen Fisher is known for its strong family policy.[29] As mentioned, Yahoo! CEO Marissa Mayer doubled her employees' maternity and paternity leave policies. Costco is also known for pro-worker policies; in fact, the company's recent increase in profits is attributed to its CEO's endorsement of minimum wage hikes in 2013.[30] And some newer trends in co-working spaces are helping bridge the work-family gap; for example, NextKids, a co-working space in San Francisco, offers on-site child care for freelancers and startups.[31] Hopefully, business leaders who do understand the benefits of pro-family policies will begin to lead the conversation. As Vicki Shabo notes, "By adding their voices to discussions about the need for these policies, business owners clearly demonstrate that the big business lobby's opposition to common-sense measures like these doesn't reflect the views of all business owners in America, especially those small business owners and corporations that understand that higher wages and supportive workplace policies are good for business."[32]

The Perils of State Child Care Support

While the business world for the most part continues to drag its feet on providing paid family leave, people who rely on state aid for their child care costs are also feeling the pinch. Child care in this country can cost upward of $15,000 annually—an expense that challenges many low- and middle-income Americans.[33] Thus, many parents are reluctant to take time off of work to care for a sick child; they fear they could lose their jobs, and the loss of income would impact their access to child care.

The National Women's Law Center studies state policies that affect access to child care subsidies for low-income Americans, including income eligibility limits to qualify for child care assistance, co-payments, reimbursement rates for child care providers, waiting lists, and eligibility for assistance for parents searching for a job. According to the center, these policies "are critical in determining families' access to childcare assistance and the extent of help they receive from that assistance."[34] Unfortunately, most states have fallen behind where they were in 2001. After the Great Recession, American Recovery and Reinvestment Act (ARRA) funds were applied to child care assistance in 2009 and 2010, but this injection of funding was temporary, and increases to federal spending on child care through the Child Care and Development Block Grant (CCDBG) have not matched what ARRA funds briefly provided.[35]

In 2013, twenty-seven states improved their access to child care for low-income people through various policies (fewer budgetary cutbacks of child care assistance programs, greater access to child care assistance for unemployed parents who are looking for a job, and fewer waiting lists for child care assistance). However, many states continue to have restrictive income criteria for child care subsidies.[36] For example, a family with an income above 150 percent of the poverty level ($29,295 for a family of three) does not qualify for assistance in fourteen states. A family with an income above 200 percent of the poverty level ($39,060 annually for a family of three) does not qualify for assistance in thirty-eight states.[37] Overall, approximately half of the states low-ered the income threshold at which families qualified for help, or kept their income limits at the same dollar amount, without any adjustment for inflation, between 2012 and 2013. Thus for people who work in the 50 percent of American jobs that pay $34,000 or less per year, covering child care expenses is a significant chal-lenge.[38]

The reductions in child care assistance are connected with the severe budget woes states have experienced in recent years (including fewer federal resources being doled out to states for child care assistance). A further issue is the block grant structure of child care assistance: the aforementioned CCDBG, and Temporary Assistance for Needy Families (TANF). Block grants allow states flexibility in how they apply the federal dollars they receive. By contrast, federal categorical grants, such as Medicaid, are given out to states with more guidelines and restrictions. TANF and CCDBG together yielded $8.17 billion in 2012—when adjusted for inflation, this comes to a bit less than 2011's child care assistance funding and about $2.5 billion less than 2001's, also adjusted for inflation. According to Karen Schulman, senior policy analyst at the National Women's Law Center, "States have flexibility and are not required to set income eligibility limits at a certain level, they're allowed to have waiting lists, and vary their child care assistance in other ways. So when resources are tight they'll pull back and leave families without assistance they used to receive. In that sense the flexibility of block grants can have a downside."[40]

To negotiate these financial difficulties with families' care needs, some states have attempted to cut costs by restricting child care assistance policies. For example, Massachusetts's waiting list for child care assistance increased 60 percent in 2012.[41] At the same time, the state slightly relaxed its income eligibility limit from the year before, enabling a family of three earning up to $42,025 to qualify for assistance. By contrast, Louisiana tightened its income eligibility limit to $35,868 for a family of three from $37,896 in 2011, but the state does not have a waiting list.[42] "States are making tradeoffs, within their child care programs as well as among many programs," Schulman says. "And all of these programs tend to help a lot of the same families."[43]

The juxtaposition of the challenges faced by families (i.e., the employers of child care workers) with those faced by the child care workers themselves presents a particularly vexing conundrum: how to offer care that is sustainable for everyone when care workers themselves are so strapped. In 2013, Sarah Jaffe wrote in Jacobin about Nancy Harvey, the director of an Oakland, California, day care center who told Jaffe that childcare providers are exempt from minimum wage requirements, and that state agencies that offer subsidies fail to pay providers for months at a time. Yet failure to be compensated doesn't stop Harvey from doing her job caring for children. "Most of us don't have any kind of health care, we don't have retirement, we don't have medical, dental, vision," Harvey said. "With the subsidized program we are entitled to ten paid holidays a year. That means if you've been in the business for five years, if you've been in the business for forty-five years, you get ten days." According to Harvey, care providers like her "don't have a voice at the table. We have people making decisions that have no concept of what it's like to walk in our shoes."[44]

Employers as Advocates for Domestic Workers

One of the most heartening aspects of the movement for domestic worker rights is the empathy and compassion more and more employers are showing for their domestic employees—feelings rooted in their shared economic struggles. Elizabeth Tang of the International Domestic Workers Federation notes that what makes the current US movement for domestic worker rights stand out from those of other nations is that despite policy frustrations, employers of domestic workers are deeply involved in helping their employees. The involvement of employers demonstrates the interconnectedness and interdependence of care recipients and those who provide care.

Progressive Jewish groups represent many employers of domestic workers, and they are among the most active employers in the current movement. Just as Jews for Racial and Economic Justice led the involvement of employers in New York's campaign for a domestic workers' bill of rights, Bend the Arc, a national Jewish group with offices in California, became active in the movement through advocating for AB 241, the California Domestic Workers' Bill of Rights. Bend the Arc formed out of two different groups: Jewish Funds for Justice and the Progressive Jewish Alliance, which together work on a variety of organizing and advocacy for progressive national issues, leadership development, grant making, and community investment.

The group had previously advocated for hotel workers' rights and then became involved in the domestic workers' bill of rights campaign. "At our 2011 membership meeting, our members voted with their feet," says David Levitus, California campaign director of Bend the Arc.[45] "And in voting with their feet, what that means is people selected the campaign they thought they'd work on personally. So we picked the AB 241 campaign. We found that the issue struck close to home. We had been considering tax and criminal justice issues, but there was an extraordinary amount of interest in the domestic workers' cause. As employers we think of ourselves as progressives, we have a special obligation and special power to do something." In 2013, Bend the Arc participated in a variety of actions, including a protest rally outside of Governor

Jerry Brown's Los Angeles office and a Mother's Day breakfast at which employers served workers. According to Levitus, Bend the Arc is "focused on the rise of caregiving as an industry."[46]

Amy Dean, co-author of *A New New Deal: How Regional Activism Will Reshape the American Labor Movement*, writes about how the organic growth of independent Jewish spiritual communities is happening parallel to the rise of domestic worker organizing and other non-unionized, low-wage worker organizing: "Both alt-labor and alt-congregations (or 'professionally-run emerging Jewish communities')…are explicitly welcoming of LGBT, interfaith, and immigrant groups/newcomers; this inclusivity makes their commitment to justice part of their fabric rather than an afterthought."[47]

Hand in Hand: The Domestic Employers Network has worked to organize employers of domestic workers; as Dean explains is happening in the Jewish community, the group is invested in the workers' economic situation. "When I first heard about Hand in Hand, I definitely had a moment of feeling like, oh my gosh, here we are working hard and money's tight, so I think when I heard the idea that we should somehow be doing more I remember a feeling of resistance, feeling like we can't afford to do more than we already do," Meg Yardley, a nanny employer and member of the group, says.[48] Then, speaking of her children's nanny, she adds, "But when I really listened and thought about it, I had to agree that it made sense from knowing Tania and Tania's mother and hearing their stories; it was clear to me how vulnerable they are in the workforce." Tania had shared with Yardley that she and her mother had held jobs in which they were required to work extremely long hours but did not feel any sense of security and, due to state policy, were ineligible for overtime.

Yardley and her husband began thinking about these issues when they joined a nanny-share. "In our nanny-share, we could have done things that were unfair because we had never been employers before, so it's a strange role to be in. I'm someone's boss now? But the nanny-share we joined had really good practices," Yardley says. "We gave sick days, vacation time, guaranteed to pay our hours every week even if the child was sick to help guarantee the worker's hours." Yardley points out the lack of job security in being a nanny, as most work for families for two to three years until the child goes to preschool, and then the nanny must find a new job. When that happens, the nanny can't count on a new employer consenting to whatever terms she agreed on with the previous one, or necessarily adhering to basic labor standards.

As people like Meg Yardley demonstrate, employer support is an important part of the domestic workers' movement—particularly given that the interests of employers and domestic workers are often portrayed in popular culture as being at odds. For example, in the 2013 film *Enough Said*, starring Julia Louis-Dreyfus, James Gandolfini, and Toni Collette, Collette's character employs an immigrant woman to clean her home and care for her children. The two spar constantly, and Collette exhibits a great deal of distrust for the woman. The worker is portrayed as haughty, cocky, and fickle, and the employer is portrayed as exasperated—a conflict that makes for an entertaining film but a careless portrayal of how hard domestic workers toil for low wages.[49]

Despite some unfortunate depictions of the worker-employer relationship, there are celebrities who have helped shift the cultural portrayal of how employers and domestic workers relate to each other—and some who have directly helped the domestic workers' movement.[50] In a public service announcement in support of California's 2012 domestic workers' bill of rights, comedian Amy Poehler said, "I am an actor, and a worker, and a working woman. Many people ask me how I balance it all. And the truth is, it wouldn't be possible for me to do all of those things without the help that I get in my home."[51]

In April 2014, Daniel Murphy of the New York Mets decided to take three days of paternity leave to be with his wife as she underwent a cesarean section.[52] Several sports commentators criticized Murphy for this decision. For example, Boomer Esiason said that Murphy should have told his wife, "[Have the] C-section before the season starts; I need to be at opening day. I'm sorry, this is what makes our money." As comments like this demonstrate, restructuring the economy to value the labor of the private sphere is a tall order, requiring significant cultural and political change.

Over the long term, however, policies that value domestic labor can affect not only wages and protections for domestic workers, but all families—particularly those who fall within lower income brackets. Policymakers trying to win support for applying tax dollars to paid leave and child care access policies face a major challenge, though some cities and states have begun to see success in this regard. Encouragingly, in an emerging trend, caregiving is slowly coming to be understood as an occupation worthy of economic and social value—in part because employers of domestic workers are becoming active in the movement for domestic workers' rights.

9.Immigration Reform, and the Continued Invisibility of Domestic Labor

"There will be a time in the very near future when there will be a shortage of caregivers. Immigration reform could be a solution to that problem. But policymakers are not thinking that far into the future."—**Nikki Brown-Booker,** activist and employer of domestic workers

With its emphasis on enforcement—deportation—over compassion—the issuing of visas—US immigration policy under the Obama administration has been hostile to immigrant workers. The deportations of more than two million undocumented people living in the United States since Obama took office in 2009 have earned the president the nickname "deporter-in-chief."[1] As MSNBC's Chris Hayes aptly noted in April 2014, "From the perspective of justice and human decency, policy on illegal immigration under this president, particularly on deportations, has been a disaster: tens of thousands of families torn apart…horror stories left and right."[2] The rash of deportations has harshly impacted domestic workers, many of whom are immigrant women.[3]

Beyond the administration's draconian deportation policy, the feeble conversation that has taken place around immigration reform at the federal level has only entrenched familiar notions about what type of labor is "productive" and therefore worthy of a visa. While the US Senate's immigration reform bill, passed in June 2013, did include some protections for immigrant workers, the legislators did not even consider visas specifically for care workers, despite a projected rise in demand for their services in the coming years.[4] As of April 2014, the House of Representatives has failed to take any action on immigration reform. If the Republican-controlled House ever does grapple with immigration policy, it is unlikely that its legislation would include the protections for immigrant women workers that the Senate supported, let alone visas for care workers.

Immigration Status and Domestic Worker Abuse

The paucity of immigration policy in this country leaves immigrant domestic workers vulnerable to abuse by employers who claim workers "owe" them for having been brought to the United States. This kind of intimidation can deter immigrant workers from reporting labor violations or even outright abuse, as current policy often fails to protect workers when their employers retaliate and report them to immigration authorities.[5]

Santosh Bhardwaj came to the United States in 2009 with her employer Prabhu Dayal and his wife to work in their home in New York City. Two years later, Bhardwaj was threatened with deportation by Dayal after she complained about breach of contract. Dayal had promised to pay Bhardwaj ten dollars per hour, plus overtime. He had also assured her that she would work in a non-abusive environment.[6] Instead, Dayal confiscated Bhardwaj's passport and required her to work more than twelve hours a day, every day. She was threatened with deportation if she did not work fast enough, or stopped working. And despite her contract, she was paid only $300 per month.[7]

Upon hearing her story, a friend Bhardwaj had met through other workers for Indian diplomats brought her to the attention of New York City Council Member Daniel Dromm, whose office referred her to the Legal Aid Society.[8] When Bhardwaj sought assistance from the society to sue Dayal for unpaid wages, Dayal bizarrely tried to wage a public attack against the worker by releasing her photograph to the press, contacting law enforcement, and calling for her deportation. Bhardwaj was able to avoid deportation with the help of the New York Legal Aid Society, as well as a private law firm. Although she managed to stay in the country, Bhardwaj was scarred by the events, which could have escalated further had there not been advocates for her to turn to.[9]

The National Immigration Law Center has researched how employers use both visa and socioeconomic status against immigrant workers.[10] Their findings reveal that labor abuses and retaliation persist against low-wage immigrant workers whose status in the United States is largely reliant on their relationship with their employer. The threat of deportation enables such abuse, as exemplified by Santosh Bhardwaj's story. Other policies also make immigrant workers vulnerable to employer retaliation.[11] E-Verify is a government website that enables employers to confirm the immigration status of new hires by cross-checking the worker's name, Social Security number, date of birth, and alien number with information held by the Social Security Administration and Department of Homeland Security records.[12] However, there have been cases of employers using E-Verify to retaliate against workers. Indeed, the National Employment Law Center found that some employers used E-Verify only after an employee complained of wage or safety violations.[13]

President Obama has called attention to some of the exploitative practices that victimize immigrant workers. In 2013, just as the federal debate over immigration reform was heating up, he said, "Often [immigrants work] in a shadow economy, a place where employers may offer them less than the minimum wage or make them work overtime without extra pay. And when that happens, it's not just bad for them, it's bad for the entire economy, because all the businesses that are trying to do the right thing—that are hiring people legally, paying a decent wage, following the rules—they are the ones who suffer."[14] Despite the president's sympathetic words, recent immigration reform efforts were not adequately informed by domestic workers' advocacy or experiences. Several of the 2013 immigration reform proposals went as far as to include legal status for DREAMers—children who fall within the Development, Relief, and Education for Alien Minors (DREAM) Act who are eligible for legal status in the United States—as well as low-wage agricultural workers.[15] Yet domestic workers continued to be excluded.[16]

In addition, while heavyweight technology companies went to bat for highly skilled and educated immigrant workers who can bring STEM (science, technology, engineering, and math) talent to the United States, this type of clout does not exist for domestic workers.[17] "A company like Apple goes to great lengths to get a programmer from abroad documents, but that programmer is not necessarily contributing to someone's day-to-day well-being," says Nikki Brown-Booker, a woman with disabilities who hires domestic workers to care for her. Based in Berkeley, California, Brown-Booker has become an advocate for domestic workers' rights. "But someone who is contributing to someone's day-to-day wellness and happiness—like my workers have for me—cannot get documents. There will be a time in the very near future when there will be a shortage of caregivers. Immigration reform could be a solution to that problem. But policymakers are not thinking that far into the future."[18]

Immigration Reform Activism

The fact that domestic workers were mainly excluded from immigration reform in 2013 was not due to inaction by the domestic workers' movement, which took an active role in the debate. The We Belong Together campaign—a joint effort of the

National Domestic Workers Alliance and the National Asian Pacific American Women's Forum—seeks "common-sense immigration reform" that will help stem the tide of deportations and empower women workers.[19] Rather than focusing on protections for domestic workers specifically, We Belong Together frames its advocacy in ways that benefit all immigrant women. The campaign's six named priorities are: (1) an inclusive path to citizenship, (2) keeping families together, (3) workers' rights protections, particularly for women, (4) protections for survivors of violence and trafficking, (5) due process and protections for families, and (6) immigrant integration.

In furtherance of these goals, domestic worker advocates visited legislators and backed specific amendments to the Senate's immigration reform legislation. In February 2013, approximately forty domestic workers traveled to Washington, DC, to meet with legislators about immigration reform. One of the domestic workers who lobbied was forty-six-year-old Silvia Lopez. Lopez lives in Fruitvale, California, a suburb of Oakland, and has been a domestic worker for twenty years. "I was really emotional from this experience, traveling to Washington, DC," she says. "I wanted to communicate to [the lawmakers] that deportations lead to family separation, and I wanted domestic workers to be recognized by Obama."[20]

Some of the issues the domestic workers brought up to legislators were those of partner abuse and mistreatment by employers. Lopez's story exemplifies the unfortunate impact of both of these issues on workers' lives. A domestic worker since she arrived in the United States from Mexico at the age of twenty-six, Lopez first worked as a nanny for a family in Los Angeles. "First I was asked to care for the kids, but slowly, slowly, I became responsible for a great deal of other work," she says. "I would wash clothes, clean bathrooms, cook for the family. It became an abusive situation."[21] Lopez was paid so poorly that she was forced to work for a clothing-washing company on the side.

At the same time she was working hard for low wages, Lopez was also being abused at home. She had met the eventual father of her two children just three months after arriving in the United States. Lopez says that like many domestic violence situations, the relationship "was okay at first" but soon became abusive. "He was verbally abusive, to the point where I didn't see any value in myself; I had low self-esteem," she says. "But I stayed with him seventeen years, until finally my daughter said to me, 'Mom, what will happen to your life if you don't get out of this?'"[22]

Sadly, Lopez's experiences are not uncommon, as many domestic workers are victims of domestic violence, a situation that is not alleviated by current immigration policies. "We've heard numerous cases of domestic workers who are survivors of DV who have called the police, and then been deported," says NDWA director Ai-jen Poo, using an abbreviation to refer to domestic violence. "As a result, many domestic workers who experience DV are afraid to access resources or even go to a shelter. All of the work to support DV survivors is completely undermined by these policies that make people afraid of getting help and speaking out."[23]

To help address this, the We Belong Together campaign backed Senator Patrick Leahy's amendment to the 2013 immigration reform bill providing work authorization for Violence Against Women Act applicants while their applications are being processed—a process that can take over a year and a half.[24] (The Violence Against Women Act, first enacted in 1994, is a major piece of federal legislation that devotes resources to investigating and prosecuting violent crimes against women.) Measures like this can increase economic security and safety for domestic violence survivors. Advocates also supported two amendments authored by Senator Al Franken, one that would help survivors of domestic violence receive public benefits and housing, and another that would prevent children from being placed in the foster care system if their parents are detained or deported.[25] Senator Richard Blumenthal of Connecticut proposed an amendment that would allow workers access to their employment records, which was also supported by We Belong Together.[26] Finally, domestic worker advocates were supportive of Senator Amy Klobuchar's amendment to protect workers from deportation when they witness and report abuse against the elders for whom they provide care, and Senator Mazie Hirono's amendment providing protections for unaccompanied children and female detainees, reducing the likelihood of abuse during processing and detention.[27]

In Senate testimony offered on March 18, 2013, Ai-jen Poo also raised the importance of an inclusive path to citizenship with no proof of employment requirement for workers like Silvia Lopez.[28] Proof of employment is frequently a challenge for domestic workers who do not receive "offer letters," are often paid in cash, and realistically may not be able to request documentation from an employer.[29] During her testimony, Poo pointed out that undocumented workers are victimized by wage and hour violations at nearly twice the rate of documented and US-born workers.[30] For example, 37 percent of undocumented workers experience minimum wage violations, as compared with 21 percent of documented workers, and 15 percent of US-born workers. The situation is even worse for women, who make up most of the domestic sector, as 47 percent of undocumented women workers experience wage and hour violations, compared with 30 percent of undocumented men.[31] Poo also discussed the importance of protection from injury, as immigrant women are more likely to experience workplace injury than women born in the United States.

The Border Security, Economic Opportunity, and Immigration Modernization Act, S.744, passed the Senate on June 27, 2013, by a vote of sixty-eight to thirty-two. Importantly, the final bill included the proposals of Senators Leahy, Blumenthal, Hirono, Klobuchar, and Franken. (The bill did exclude one Hirono-sponsored amendment that the We Belong Together campaign had supported, which would have granted additional visas to immigrant families who experience particular hardship as a result of deportation.)[32] S.744 was seen as a positive step by the National Domestic Workers Alliance. As Ai-jen Poo said in a statement:

> The Senate has taken a big step forward toward immigration reform. The bill they passed contains a road map to citizenship for millions of families—including domestic workers. Thanks to the efforts of women around the country, and the leadership of women members of the Senate, it includes unprecedented, important measures to safeguard and include women, workers and families…. This vote for immigration reform is a vote for love, family and the future.[33]

However, some immigrant rights advocates were critical of the Senate bill. Writer Veronica Bayetti Flores pointed out that the Corker-Hoeven Amendment to S.744 blocked people who were on the legislation's required fifteen-year path to citizenship from obtaining public benefits like Medicaid.[34] The amendment also placed "unprecedented resources on the [US-Mexico] border to stem the flow of illegal immigration," according to a press release posted on the website of Senator John Hoeven of North Dakota, one of the sponsors of the amendment. Among these resources were "20,000 border patrol agents on the southern border in addition to the 18,500 agents already stationed there" as well as 350 miles of fencing—in addition to the 350 miles that were already there.[35] Of particular concern to domestic worker advocates were provisions in the amendment "which ensure that Registered Provisional Immigrants (RPIs) cannot receive green cards until at least 10 years after the enactment of the bill."[36] Jessica González-Rojas, executive director of the National Latina Institute for Reproductive Health, sharply criticized another element of the legislation:

> The Corker-Hoeven Amendment, and the underlying bill (S.744)...create an unacceptable second-class status for legalizing immigrants. Under the Senate bill, woman and families navigating the complex roadmap to citizenship would be working, paying taxes, fees, and fines, learning English, and fulfilling other requirements for 15 years or more before affordable health coverage options would become available to them. That's 15 years paying into Medicaid and other health programs without any opportunity to benefit from those same programs.[37]

No Visas for Caregivers

Workers who toil as caregivers are typically women of color earning low wages, and despite intense domestic worker activism, their voices remain largely unheard in the immigration debate. This is especially troubling when one considers the fact that demand for direct-care workers is expected to increase 48 percent over the next decade. In 2011, baby boomers in this country began to turn sixty-five at an alarming rate—one person every eight seconds. By 2030, nearly seventy-five million Americans will have reached retirement age.[39] The caregivers for this population are disproportionately going to be immigrant women. (Currently, 90 percent of in-home health care workers in the United States are female, and 56 percent are from a minority racial or ethnic group.)[40] As a basis of comparison, the population of US-born workers is expected to grow by only about 1 percent during the same time period. [41]

Despite these growing numbers, fewer than 30 percent of all employment visas are given to women as principal holders, even though industries like care work, which are projecting severe labor shortages, are dominated by women.[42] Three-quarters of dependent visa holders in the employment category are women who have the same level of education as native-born women but do not have the opportunity to work and contribute their skills to their new country.[43] "This is a waste of their talents and leads to unhealthy dependency on husbands who can and do take advantage with emotional and physical violence," Ai-jen Poo told the Senate Judiciary Committee in 2013.[44]

In 2013, the Institute for Women's Policy Research issued a report recommending improved visa access for in-home care workers as a way of promoting job mobility as well as empowering workers not to feel beholden to employers.[45] Ai-jen Poo and other domestic workers' movement leaders advocated for this as well.[46] The proposals ultimately did not resonate, however, as S.744 included no provisions for visas for caregivers.

Advocates also pursued other strategies for protecting immigrant women, including the granting of visas to people married to H-1B visa holders. The H-1B visa grants "highly skilled" workers temporary legal status; more than 70 percent of all H-1B visa holders are men.[47] At the urging of domestic worker and immigrant rights advocates, in April 2014, the White House issued an executive action authorizing employment for spouses of some H-1B visa holders.[48] This action resulted in part from Women's Fast for Families, a month-long series of fasts sponsored by the We Belong Together campaign. We Belong Together lauded the

White House's action, noting, "It is an important step towards recognizing the value of women immigrants and their contributions to this country's workforce and towards addressing the increased domestic violence endured by women immigrants whose ability to stay in the US is solely dependent on their spouses' status."

Beyond piecemeal executive actions such as the H-1B visas, however, little progress has been made on comprehensive immigration reform. After the Senate bill passed in 2013, immigration reform stalled. The House of Representatives has taken no action on immigration reform at all; House majority leader John Boehner has not only rejected the Senate bill, he has failed to lead the House toward any alternative legislation.[49] President Obama's commitment to mass deportation seems to be the only action the federal government is taking with respect to immigration policy.

Overall, the record number of deportations has come to dominate the conversation around immigration, and any discussion of comprehensive reform and a pathway to citizenship for the more than eleven million undocumented Americans living in the United States remains stymied by the House of Representatives. This failure of political leadership is extremely damaging to domestic workers, as it ignores the important contributions they make to our society. Ideally, U.S. immigration policy should aim not only to bring the brightest talent into this country, but to empower workers who are vulnerable to abuse by employers. The current conversation around immigration reform does not address the issues immigrant workers face, however. As Silvia Lopez points out, "We can't just recognize immigrants with very high education. Domestic workers are critical for the economy, too."

Conclusion and Policy Recommendations: Past, Present and Future

"All labor that uplifts humanity has dignity and importance."—**Martin Luther King Jr.**

While the domestic workers' movement achieved early success at the state level, there has now been major progress at the federal level, too. Significantly, the Fair Labor Standards Act has now been reformed to include live-in domestic workers within federal minimum wage and overtime protections. This change occurred only after an initial setback in the Supreme Court in 2007; the domestic workers' movement overcame this setback by finding allies in the Obama administration. Taking their message to the Department of Labor and the White House, domestic workers were able to change a century of policy that rendered the work of millions of live-in caregivers invisible. The efforts of these activists offer a powerful blueprint for how the domestic workers' movement can successfully move forward in future years to achieve its aims.

The Test Case

Born in Jamaica on Christmas Day, 1934, Evelyn Coke worked in home care in her native country, and stayed in the field when she came to the United States in 1970. She settled in Queens, New York, buying a small home where she lived until she passed away in 2009. As the *New York Times* noted in her obituary, Coke had been forced to stop working after she was hit by a car in 2001—an incident that led her to challenge a longstanding federal rule against paying home care workers overtime. When Coke saw a lawyer about the injuries she sustained, he reviewed her pay stubs and learned that she had spent her career often working upward of seventy hours a week, without receiving overtime. He urged her to file suit to challenge the overtime law in 2002, and she assented[1]

Though the 1974 amendment to the Fair Labor Standards Act extended overtime and minimum wage standards to cover some domestic workers, the law still exempted employees engaged in companionship services. The Department of Labor had a regulation applying the companionship exemption, the effect of which was that many live-in caregivers were still excluded from the law.[2] The exemption states in part, "Live-in domestic service employees who are employed by an employer or agency other than the family or household using their services are exempt from the Act's overtime requirements."[3] The companionship exemption denied overtime coverage to the more than two million care workers employed by home care agencies in the United States—the vast majority of whom are women of color.[4] The agency that had last employed Evelyn Coke, Long Island Care in Westbury, New York, argued that it would have suffered "tremendous and unsustainable losses" if required to pay overtime under federal law. The city of New York agreed, submitting an amicus brief stating that overtime payments to home aides could increase Medicaid costs by $250 million a year and could lead to service cuts.[5]

Coke's case was heard by the Second Circuit Court of Appeals, which held that the companionship exemption was unlawful as it defied the purpose of the FLSA—which was to expand overtime coverage to more workers—and thus was not due deference typically given to federal regulations. The case was appealed to the Supreme Court. "I hope they try to help me because I need help bad," Coke said in April 2007, after listening to oral arguments before the Court.[6] However, the Supreme Court unanimously rejected Coke's claims, ruling that the regulation excluding domestic workers was "valid and binding."[7] The Court's decision focused on the narrow question of whether the regulation is due deference, and included practically no discussion of Coke and her work. "That's the thing about advocacy like this," Coke's lawyer, Craig Becker, says. "There are many things one may have wanted to say about the worker that were outside the bounds of appropriate argument as the question before the court was a narrow question of administrative law."[8] In the wake of the verdict against her, Coke told the *Associated Press*, "I feel robbed. I feel glad it's come to everybody's attention; people are supposed to get paid when they work."[9]

Evelyn Coke passed away from heart failure in 2009, after suffering from several ailments in the final years of her life, including kidney failure, which required her to be on dialysis.[10] In a cruel irony, toward the end of her life—after a long career caring for countless elder Americans—Coke could not afford to hire a caregiver for herself.[11] Despite this, Coke never became bitter about her choice of profession. "I don't regret taking care of old people," she said.

Allies in the Executive Branch

In 2013, US Secretary of Labor Hilda Solis resigned after having served in the role since the beginning of President Obama's first term.[12] During her tenure, Solis collaborated with domestic workers' advocates to develop the regulations that would apply federal minimum wage and overtime laws to live-in domestic workers. While a number of candidates were considered for Solis's post when she resigned, Obama ultimately chose Tom Perez of the Justice Department, who also served on the board of Casa de Maryland and is considered to be an ally of workers' rights. In response to Perez's appointment, Casa de Maryland noted, "Workers in America are lucky to have an advocate and change-maker like Tom as Secretary of Labor."[13]

Three months after Perez was confirmed, Evelyn Coke's efforts finally reaped rewards: on September 17, 2013, the US Department of Labor approved regulations extending wage and overtime protections to live-in care workers.[14] The new rules, which take effect in 2015 and apply to home care workers who are hired by agencies, will mean that aides or companions who provide care work for 20 percent or more of the total hours they work in a week now fall within minimum wage and overtime protections.[15] Domestic workers and other employment rights advocates were thrilled by this outcome. Sarah Leberstein, staff attorney with the National Employment Law Project, says, "Our initial analysis is that the revised rules will result in the extension of federal minimum wage and overtime rights to the vast majority of home care workers, which is what we had hoped for."[16]

The passage of the new regulations was just part of the Obama administration's push to change many existing practices to benefit low-wage workers. In March 2014, the president issued an executive order "updating and modernizing" overtime regulations across a number of sectors.[17] Currently, many workers in executive, administrative, and professional jobs fall under "white collar exemptions" and are denied overtime. The new regulations will narrow the categories of employees that fall within these white collar exemptions. The new overtime regulations also raise the salary threshold: Right now, workers earning more than $23,660 a year can be exempt from overtime. This income threshold is nearly forty years old, and $23,660 isn't enough to pay rent in most parts of the country. The Economic Policy Institute pointed out that some ten million workers, including "insurance clerks, secretaries, low-level managers, social workers, bookkeepers, dispatchers, sales and marketing assistants, and employees in scores of other occupations," will benefit from these new regulations.[18]

One question is how the new regulations extending overtime protections to in-home care workers will impact California's In-Home Supportive Services (IHSS) program, which pays caregivers with state funds when persons with disabilities cannot afford to. IHSS celebrated its fortieth anniversary in 2013, and is the biggest attendant-services program in the country, enabling 420,000 low-income, disabled Californians to get services.[19] IHSS provides a mix of personal and domestic assistance, allowing California to maintain a relatively low number of nursing home beds per capita.[20] Some believe that the new regulations could cause the costs of this program to increase up to $250 million per year, which could result in limitations and breaks in IHSS services, and could also force the state to lay off some home care workers. "Our state's fiscal picture is better now than it has been for a number of years but is by no means fantastic," says Karen Keesler, executive director of the California Association of Public Authorities, the entity that manages the IHSS program. "Nobody argues that home care workers shouldn't get paid more in a perfect world—but we're not in a perfect world."[21] According to Keesler, the cost of the program could cause a limit to be placed on the number of hours a worker could be compensated—meaning that consumers would have to hire additional workers. "It raises a huge continuity-of-care issue," she says. "Over 70 percent of IHSS workers are family members who live with the consumer and they would all be subject to the overtime provision." To address this concern, in March 2014, California governor Jerry Brown sought to cap IHSS workers' hours to avoid having to pay them overtime.[22]

However, not everyone agrees that limiting worker hours would cause such hardships. Nikki Brown-Booker sees an upside in the possibility that the overtime requirement could lead to the hiring of more workers. "Like any employer that doesn't want to pay overtime they can alter hours of workers," she says. "If you have a few people to cover a few shifts, you won't have to pay overtime and you may be adding people to the system."[23]

The Future of the Domestic Workers' Movement

The extending of overtime benefits to live-in caregivers is one of the most critical reforms that the domestic workers' movement has helped achieve in the past decade. For much of our country's history, domestic workers have had to labor under poor economic conditions, in isolation from their peers and colleagues, under an archaic political and legal system that refused to recognize their value. Unlike the "public sphere" where—with some important exceptions[24]—work environments are generally regulated for safety and workers are paid according to basic standards, the "domestic sphere" was always part of the informal economy, an underworld where reproductive labor was devalued and deemed unworthy of protection.

However, all of this is changing, as the growing domestic workers' movement conveys the message that domestic labor is worthy of dignity and respect. As activism around conditions of low pay, wage theft, and mistreatment and abuse of workers has increased across multiple sectors, the domestic workers' movement has been able to weave a relatable narrative about the plight of being a worker in today's economy.

Despite progress on the organizing and policy fronts, domestic workers still face resistance from legislators in some states who do not believe in offering basic protections such as overtime. The exclusion of domestic workers from such basic protections has been so systemic for so long that bringing them out of the shadows is, according to some policymakers, just not a priority. This persistently unfriendly policy environment is particularly unfortunate given that domestic workers are so vital to the lives of the sick and the growing numbers of elderly in the United States.

In light of this resistance, there is still much work to do. The following are important policy changes and actions that will help make sure that the contributions of domestic workers are truly valued:

Fund Immigrant Community Organizers and Domestic Workers' Groups

It is crucial that community organizations such as MUA, Casa de Maryland, and Domestic Workers United have needed resources and support to aid workers who are facing exploitation or mistreatment. One of the most important factors in the domestic workers' movement's continued success will be the ability of these groups to develop and maintain deep ties with specific communities of workers. The Fair Food Program in Florida is a key example of how tightly organizers can be integrated with the communities they serve. Adhikaar, Matahari: Eye of the Day, and other groups that are part of the National Domestic Workers Alliance are not only protecting and empowering women but they are also fulfilling the crucial (and under-resourced) objective of cultivating a stronger future US workforce. And the resources these groups generate to date helps US activists make an impact for domestic workers in the US and also abroad, as evidenced by NDWA's advocacy at the International Labor Organization. These groups are helping workers understand how to negotiate for better wages, build confidence in the workplace, collaborate with supervisors and clients, and professionalize the domestic work sector. Without robust community organizations acting as watchdogs and advocates, the public would have no idea of the kind of domestic worker abuse that takes place.

Reform Diplomatic Immunity

In late 2013, domestic worker Sangeeta Richard's allegations of mistreatment against Indian diplomat Devyani Khobragade drew national attention. Richard alleged that she was denied a minimum wage to which she is entitled as a worker in the United States. The Indian government argued that Khobragade should not be charged with any wrongdoing because her position with the government immunized her from prosecution.[25] This case demonstrates the continuing need for special protections for domestic workers who labor for diplomats. Many domestic workers who are abused, mistreated, or trafficked are subject to the whims of foreign dignitaries who are not likely to be held accountable under any nation's labor laws. Current law holds serving diplomats immune from civil and criminal prosecution when they are accused of abusing their workers. Increased accountability of sitting diplomats, perhaps through an expansion of the commercial activities exception to diplomatic immunity, would help domestic workers who have been trafficked or abused by their diplomat employers.

Increase Visas for Domestic Workers

The 2013 immigration legislation passed in the US Senate did include some protections for immigrant women, such as Senator Leahy's amendment providing work authorization for victims of violence. Overall, however, the immigration reform conversation did little to help broaden what type of labor is deemed valuable—even while the United States faces a growing aging population and higher demand for care workers. Debate over immigration reform has stalled since 2013, but if it does resume, Congress should consider increasing the number of visas for immigrants who will be filling caregiving positions.

Improve Paid Family Leave Policies

Most families in the United States do not have access to paid family leave. Being able to take time off from work to care for children and ill or elderly family members is critical. Unfortunately, this labor is not viewed as worthwhile or productive—only because it doesn't directly benefit business. Both policymakers and employers should prioritize paid family leave; more states should enact paid family leave programs such as those enacted in California, New Jersey, and Rhode Island. Enacting a paid family leave program at the federal level would help ensure that all US workers have some level of economic security while they engage in care work for brief periods of time.

Continue Ensuring that Labor Law and Policy Includes Domestic Workers

The primary policy focus of this book is that in the context of labor laws, domestic workers have historically not been on equal footing with all other workers. It has been a failure of our democracy to exclude domestic workers from labor laws for so long, to treat domestic workers as if they do not matter, as if the contribution they make to our economy, families, and communities by tirelessly caring for our young, ill, infirm, and aging is not worthy of the protections to which most other workers are entitled. As Eileen Boris and Jennifer Klein have noted, "These workers are America's frontline caregivers."[26] Resistance to including domestic workers within labor protections bespeaks an inadequate investment in the future of a critical and in-demand sector.

Slowly, because of the women at the helm of the domestic workers' movement—powerful, strong women like Priscilla Gonzalez, who led Domestic Workers' United for ten years, Andrea Cristina Mercado, Maria Distancia and Juana Flores of Mujeres Unidas y Activas, Ai-jen Poo and Barbara Young of the National

Domestic Workers' Alliance, Natalicia Tracy of the Brazilian Immigrant Center, Sarita Gupta of Jobs with Justice, Luna Ranjit of Adhikaar, Marci Seville, Hina Shah and, Rocio Avila of the Golden Gate School of Law Women's Employment Rights Clinic, , and many, many others—the legal and cultural paradigm is beginning to shift. "Through the domestic workers' movement, we are blazing a trail where there had been none," Priscilla Gonzalez says. "We're doing it differently, and we're winning."[27]

Acknowledgements

Ai-jen Poo and everyone at the National Domestic Workers' Alliance who generously engaged with me in better understanding their important work; everyone at Hand in Hand; Jobs with Justice; Sarita Gupta; Luna Ranjit; Marci Seville; Lydia Edwards; Rocio Avia; Gayle Kirshenbaum; everyone at Bend the Arc; Mercy Albaran; Natalicia Tracy.

Most of all, my family and friends for their undying support.

Notes

Introduction

1. Fatima Cortessi (domestic worker), interview by author, June 5, 2013.
2. Ibid.
3. Rebecca Burns, "Domestic Insurgents," *In These Times*, April 1, 2013, http://inthesetimes.com/article/14731/domestic_insurgents/.
4. Meg Yardley, Hand in Hand, interview by author, July 7, 2013.
5. International Labour Organization, *Domestic Workers across the World: Global and Regional Statistics and the Extent of Legal Protection* (Geneva: International Labour Office, 2013).
6. Bryce Covert, "The Global Domestic Workforce is Enormous—and Very Vulnerable," *Nation*, January 10, 2013, http://www.thenation.com/blog/172099/global-domestic-workforce-enormous-and-very-vulnerable.
7. International Labour Organization, *Domestic Workers across the World*.
8. Laura Dresser, "Cleaning and Caring in the Home: Shared Problems? Shared Possibilities?" in T*he Gloves-Off Economy: Workplace Standards at the Bottom of America's Labor Market*, eds. Annette Bernhardt et al. (Champaign: University of Illinois, Champaign-Urbana, 2008).
9. Sheila Bapat, "Finally, Domestic Workers Get Basic Labor Protections," *RH Reality Check*, October 18, 2013, http://rhrealitycheck.org/article/2013/09/18/finally-domestic-workers-get-basic-labor-protections/.
10. International Labour Organization Convention on Decent Work for Domestic Workers (C. 189).
11. Gender across Borders, "Globalization and the Commodification of Female Domestic Work," April 3, 2012, http://www.genderacrossborders.com/2012/04/03/globalization-and-the-commodification-of-female-domestic-work/.
12. Linda Burnham and Nik Theodore, "Home Economics: The Invisible and Unregulated World of Domestic Work," National Domestic Workers Alliance, 2012, http://gender.stanford.edu/sites/default/files/HomeEconomicsEnglish.pdf
13. Burnham and Theodore, "Home Economics," 9.
14. Sarah Jaffe, "Trickle-Down Feminism," *Dissent*, Winter 2013, http://

www.dissentmagazine.org/article/trickle-down-feminism.
15. Burns, "Domestic Insurgents."
16. Mariarosa Dalla Costa and Selma James, *The Power of Women and the Subversion of Community,* 1972, http://libcom.org/library/power-women-subversion-community-della-costa-selma-james.
17. Ibid.
18. Barbara Ehrenreich, "Maid to Order," *Harpers,* April 1, 2000, http://harpers.org/archive/2000/04/maid-to-order/.
19. Gloria Steinem, "Revaluing Economics," in *Moving Beyond Words* (New York: Open Road Integrated Media, 1994).
20. Gender across Borders, "Globalization and the Commodification of Female Domestic Work."
21. V. Spike Peterson, "Plural Processes, Patterned Connections," *Globalizations* 1, no. 1 (2004): 50–68.
22. Ibid.
23. Angela P. Harris, "From Stonewall to the Suburbs?: Toward a Political Economy of Sexuality," *William & Mary Bill of Rights Journal* 14, no. 4 (2006): 1539–82.
24. Terri Nilliasca, "Some Women's Work: Domestic Work, Race, Class, Heteropatriarchy, and the Limits of Legal Reform," *Michigan Journal of Race and Law* 16 (2011): 377.
25. Janie A. Chuang, "Achieving Accountability for Migrant Domestic Workers," *University of North Carolina Law Review Symposium* (2010): 1641.
26. Priscilla Gonzalez, telephone interview by author, San Francisco, CA, April 6, 2013.

1. Slavery and Domestic Work–Then and Now

1. Harriet Jacobs, *Incidents in the Life of a Slave Girl* (North Carolina: University of North Carolina Chapel Hill, 2003), http://docsouth.unc.edu/fpn/jacobs/jacobs.html.
2. Catherine Lavender, "Slavery in the Southern Gender System," City University of New York, Spring 2009.
3. Remeike Forbes, "Why Django Can't Revolt," Jacobin, January 2013, http://jacobinmag.com/2013/01/why-django-cant-revolt/.
4. Jacobs, *Incidents in the Life of a Slave Girl.*
5. Lavender, "Slavery in the Southern Gender System."
6. Ibid.
7. Burnham and Theodore, "Home Economics."

8. Paul Finkelman, "Defining Slavery Under a 'Government Instituted for the Protection of the Rights of Mankind,'" *Hamline Law Review* 35 (2012): 551–90.

9. Act XIII, 2 Laws of Virginia 440 (Hening 1823), enacted December 1662.

10. Hina Shah and Marci Seville, "Domestic Worker Organizing: Building a Contemporary Movement for Dignity and Power," *Albany Law Review* 75 (2012): 416.

11. Ibid., 416–17.

12. Nilliasca, "Some Women's Work," 377.

13. Gurung v. Malhotra, 851 F.Supp. 2d 583 (SDNY 2012).

14. Ibid.

15. Amy Tai, telephone interview by author, Washington, DC, February 17, 2013.

16. "U.S. Government's Efforts to Address Alleged Abuse of Household Workers by Foreign Diplomats with Immunity Could Be Strengthened," US Government Accountability Office (2008).

17. *Diplomatic Relations Act*, Pub. L. 95-393, 90th Congress, 2nd Sess. (1969).

18. Ivy Suriyopas, telephone interview by author, New York, NY, June 4, 2013.

19. Chuang, "Achieving Accountability for Migrant Domestic Workers," 1643–44.

20. Ibid.

21. "Hidden in the Home: Abuse of Domestic Workers with Special Visas in the United States," Human Rights Watch (2001), www.hrw.org/reports/2001/usadom/.

22. *Alien Contract Labor Act*, 48th Cong., 2nd Sess. (1885), http://library.uwb.edu/guides/usimmigration/1885_contract_labor_law.html

23. Edward P. Hutchinson, *Legislative History of American Immigration Policy, 1798–1965* (Philadelphia: University of Pennsylvania Press, 1981).

24. Josh Eidelson, "Guest Workers as Bellwether," *Dissent*, Spring 2013, http://www.dissentmagazine.org/article/guest-workers-as-bellwether.

25. Tayyab Mahmud, "Cheaper Than a Slave: Indentured Labor, Colonialism and Capitalism," *Whittier Law Review* 34 (2012).

26. International Labour Organization, *ILO Global Estimate of Forced Labour 2012*, http://www.ilo.org/wcmsp5/groups/public/—ed_norm/—declaration/documents/publication/wcms_182004.pdf.

27. California Department of Justice, The State of Human Trafficking in California (2012): 17, http://oag.ca.gov/sites/all/files/pdfs/ht/human-

trafficking-2012.pdf.

28. Ibid.

29. California Department of Justice, *The State of Human Trafficking in California*, 17.

30. Ibid.

31. Patrick Belser, "Forced Labor and Human Trafficking: Estimating the Profits" (paper for International Labor Office, Geneva, 2005): 18.

32. Tiffany Williams, "Human Trafficking Awareness Day: Spotlight on Domestic Workers," *Huffington Post*, January 10, 2013, http://www.huffingtonpost.com/tiffany-williams/human-trafficking-awarene_b_2443886.html.

33. *Diplomatic Relations Act*, Pub. L. 95¬–393, 90th Congress, 2nd Sess. (1969).

34. Ibid.

35. Ibid.

36. Jean Bruggeman and Elizabeth Keyes, "Meeting the Legal Needs of Human Trafficking Victims: An Introduction for Domestic Violence Attorneys and Advocates," American Bar Association (2009), http://www.americanbar.org/content/dam/aba/migrated/2011_build/domestic_violence/dv_trafficking.authcheckdam.pdf.

37. Jennifer Hoover Kappus, "Does Immunity Mean Impunity? The Legal and Political Battle of Household Workers Against Trafficking and Exploitation by Their Foreign Diplomat Employers," *Case Western Law Review* 61 (2010): 269–307.

38. Ibid.

39. Ibid.

40. US Department of State, "U.S. Laws on Trafficking in Persons," http://www.state.gov/j/tip/laws/.

41. *Trafficking and Violence Protection Act*, 2000, Pub. L. No. 106–386, 106th Cong., 2nd Sess. (October 28, 2000), US Department of State.

42. Chuang, "Achieving Accountability for Migrant Domestic Workers," 1647.

43. "2013 State Ratings on Human Trafficking Laws," Polaris Project, http://www.polarisproject.org/what-we-do/policy-advocacy/national-policy/state-ratings-on-human-trafficking-laws.

44. Tiffany Williams, in-person interview by author, Washington, DC, February 11, 2013.

45. Rocio Avila. In-person interview by author. San Francisco, CA, February 1, 2013

46. "Beyond Survival," National Domestic Workers Alliance, http://www.

domesticworkers.org/beyondsurvival.

47. Brigitte Amiri, telephone interview by author, San Francisco, CA, March 8, 2013.

48. Tiffany Williams, interview.

49. American Civil Liberties Union of Massachusetts v. Sebelius, 697 F.Supp.2d 200 (2010).

50. Appellate Brief, American Civil Liberties Union of Massachusetts (ACLUM) v. United States Conference of Catholic Bishops and Kathleen Sebelius, filed October 18, 2012.

2. "No Deal" for Domestic Workers: Activism Before, During, and After the New Deal

1. Peggie R. Smith, "Regulating Paid Household Work: Class, Gender, Race, and Agendas of Reform," *American University Law Review* 48, no. 4 (1999): 891.

2. "Black Women Advance Labor's Cause in an Unlikely Setting: 1881 Atlanta," American Postal Workers Union, February 2010, http://www.apwu.org/laborhistory/10-1_atlantawomen/10-1_atlantawomen.htm.

3. Ibid.

4. Ibid.

5. Ibid.

6. Tera W. Hunter, *To 'Joy My Freedom: Southern Black Women's Lives and Labors after the Civil War* (Cambridge: Harvard University Press, 1998).

7. Shah and Seville, "Domestic Worker Organizing," 461.

8. Donna L. Van Raaphorst, *Union Maids Not Wanted: Organizing Domestic Workers 1870–1940* (Praeger, 1988).

9. "The Domestic Workers Union," National Women's History Museum, http://www.nwhm.org/online-exhibits/industry/DWU.htm.

10. Shah and Seville, "Domestic Worker Organizing," 421.

11. Ibid., 422.

12. Ibid., 424.

13. Ibid., 422.

14. Ibid.

15. Ibid.

16. William L. Niemi and David J. Plante, "The Search for the Meaning of the New Deal: Creating a Democratic Political Economy," prepared for APSA annual meeting (2010): 10.

17. Ibid., 2.

18. Juan Perea, "The Echoes of Slavery: Recognizing the Racist Origins of the Agricultural and Domestic Worker Exclusion from the National

Labor Relations Act," *Ohio State Law Journal* 71, no. 1 (2011): 117. The quotation is taken from John P. Davis's testimony on the Social Security Act of 1935.

19. Phyllis Palmer, *Domesticity and Dirt: Housewives and Domestic Servants in the United States, 1920–1945*, Women in the Political Economy (Philadelphia, Temple University Press: 1991).

20. *National Labor Relations Act*, Pub. L. 74–198, 74th Congress, 2nd Session (1935).

21. Ibid.

22. Josh Eidelson, "Workers, and the NLRB, Under Attack," *Nation*, March 5, 2012, http://www.thenation.com/article/166606/workers-and-nlrb-under-attack#.

23. *National Labor Relations Act*, Pub. L. 74–198, 74th Congress, 2nd Session (1935).

24. Perea, "The Echoes of Slavery," 120.

25. Kenneth M. Casebeer, "Drafting Wagner's Act: Leon Keyserling and the Precommittee Drafts of the Labor Disputes Act and the National Labor Relations Act," *Industrial Relations Law Journal* 73 (1989): 114.

26. *National Labor Relations Act*, Pub. L. 74–198, 74th Congress, 2nd Session (1935).

27. Ibid.

28. Perea, "The Echoes of Slavery," 99.

29. Ibid., 119.

30. Ibid., 120.

31. Shah and Seville, "Domestic Worker Organizing," 424.

32. Ibid.

33. Perea, "The Echoes of Slavery," 115.

34. Ibid, 115.

35. Ibid., 116.

36. Ibid, 116.

37. *Civil Rights Act*. Pub. L. 88–352, 88th Cong, 1st Session (1964), http://www.eeoc.gov/laws/statutes/titlevii.cfm.

38. Maggie Caldwell, "Invisible Women: The Real History of Domestic Workers in America," *Mother Jones*, February 7, 2013, http://www.motherjones.com/politics/2013/02/timeline-domestic-workers-invisible-history-america.

39. Eileen Boris and Jennifer Klein, *Caring for America: Home Health Workers in the Shadow of the Welfare State* (New York: Oxford University Press, 2012).

40. *Fair Labor Standards Act*. Pub. L. 75–718, 75th Cong, 2nd Session

(1938).

41. Boris and Klein, *Caring for America.*

42. *Fair Labor Standards Amendments of 1974.* Pub. L. No. 93–259, 93rd Cong., 2nd Session (1974).

43. Ibid. A Department of Labor fact sheet states, "'Companionship services' means services for the care, fellowship, and protection of persons who because of advanced age or physical or mental infirmity cannot care for themselves. Such services include household work for aged or infirm persons including meal preparation, bed making, clothes washing and other similar personal services. General household work is also included, as long as it does not exceed 20 percent of the total weekly hours worked by the companion. Where this 20 percent limitation is exceeded, the employee must be paid for all hours in compliance with the minimum wage and overtime requirements of the FLSA."

44. Shah and Seville, "Domestic Worker Organizing," 424.

45. Boris and Klein, *Caring for America.*

46. Dalla Costa and James, *The Power of Women and the Subversion of Community.*

47. Ibid.

48. Selma James. "Women, the Unions, and Work, or...what is not to be done." National Conference of Women at Manchester March 25-26. 1972, p. 4.

49. Boris and Klein, *Caring for America.*

50. Ibid.

3. Triumph in New York

1. Stacey Vanek Smith, "Nannies Get New Rights in N.Y.C. Measure," *Christian Science Monitor,* May 16, 2003, http://www.csmonitor.com/2003/0516/p02s01-usgn.html.

2. "Governor Paterson Signs Domestic Workers Bill of Rights," New York Governor Website, August 31, 2010, http://www.governor.ny.gov/archive/paterson/press/08312010DWBOR.html.

3. Barbara Young, telephone interview by author, San Francisco, CA, December 11, 2012.

4. Kemeng Kai, Anna Laura Bennett, and Laine Middaugh, "Domestic Workers' Movement in New York," May 2, 2012.

5. Priscilla Gonzalez, interview.

6. Domestic Workers United, NDWA, Urban Justice Center, *Domestic Workers and Collective Bargaining: A Proposal for Immediate Inclusion*

of Domestic Workers in the New York State Labor Relations Act (October 2010).

7. Ibid.

8. Smith, "Nannies Get New Rights in N.Y.C. Measure."

9. Local Law 2006, Domestic Workers' Rights, www.nassaucountyny.gov/ agencies/HRC/Docs/PDF/Local_Law-2006-Domestic_Workers_ Rights.pdf.

10. American Worker Cooperative, "Unity Housecleaners," January 24, 2011, http://www.american.coop/node/273.

11. Kai, Bennett, and Middaugh, "Domestic Workers' Movement in New York."

12. Ibid.

13. Barbara Ehrenreich, "The Nannies' Norma Rae," *New York Times Style*, April 26, 2011, http://tmagazine.blogs.nytimes.com/2011/04/26/the-nannies-norma-rae.

14. Reva Siegel, "The Jurisgenerative Role of Social Movements in United States Constitutional Law," *Yale Law Review* (2004).

15. Ibid.

16. Gayle Kirshenbaum, in-person interview by author, New York, NY, February 13, 2013.

17. Gayle Kirshenbaum, interview.

18. Ai-jen Poo, *Organizing with Love: Lessons from the New York Domestic Workers Bill of Rights Campaign* (Ann Arbor: Center for the Education of Women, University of Michigan, 2010).

19. Luna Ranjit, telephone interview by author. San Francisco, CA, December 30, 2012

20. Richard Winsten, telephone interview by author, San Francisco, CA, February 22, 2013.

21. Priscilla Gonzalez, interview.

22. Richard Winsten, interview.

23. New York State Assembly, A01470 floor debate, July 1, 2010.

24. Rahul Saksena, "New York Closes in on a Domestic Workers Bill of Rights" *Blog of Rights*, ACLU, June 2, 2010, http://www.aclu.org/blog/ human-rights-immigrants-rights-womens-rights/new-york-closes-domestic-workers-bill-rights.

25. New York State Assembly, A01470 votes, July 1, 2010, http://assembly. state.ny.us/leg/?default_fld=&bn=A01470&term=2009&Summary=Y &Votes=Y.

26. National Employment Law Project and Domestic Workers United, *Rights Begin at Home: Protecting Yourself as a Domestic Worker* (Novem-

ber 2010), http://www.nelp.org/page/-/Justice/2011/RightsBeginatHome.pdf?nocdn=1.

27. Ibid.

28. Ibid.

29. Ibid.

30. Ibid.

31. Domestic Workers United, NDWA, and Urban Justice Center, *Domestic Workers and Collective Bargaining.*

32. Kirk Semple, "Few Domestic Workers Know about Laws Protecting Them," *New York Times*, April 14, 2011.

33. Sharon Lerner, "The Uphill Battle to Enforce Domestic Workers' Rights," *Nation*, June 12, 2012, http://www.thenation.com/article/168353/uphill-battle-enforce-domestic-workers-rights.

34. *The Park Slope Parents Nanny Compensation Survey 2011*, http://www.parkslopeparents.com/Nanny-101/the-park-slope-parents-nanny-survey-results.html.

35. Ibid.

36. Hollis Pfitsch, email interview by author, San Francisco, CA, May 2, 2013.

37. Stephanie Breedlove, telephone interview by author, San Francisco, CA, January 21, 2014.

4. Heartbreak in California

1. Mark Engler, "Ai-jen Poo: Organizing Labor—with Love," *Yes!*, November 29, 2011, http://www.yesmagazine.org/issues/the-yes-breakthrough-15/ai-jen-poo-organizing-labor-with-love.

2. Kathleen Miles, "Domestic Workers Bill in California Brings Housekeepers and Nannies to the Streets," *Huffington Post*, March 7, 2013, http://www.huffingtonpost.com/2013/03/07/domestic-workers-california-bill_n_2822520.html.

3. Ibid.

4. National Domestic Workers Alliance, Data Center, Center for Urban Economic Development, University of Illinois at Chicago, *Home Truths: Domestic Workers in California*, May 29, 2013, http://www.domesticworkers.org/sites/default/files/HomeTruths.pdf.

5. National Domestic Workers Alliance, "A Message about the California Domestic Worker Bill of Rights Veto," October 2, 2012, http://www.domesticworkers.org/news/2012/a-message-about-the-california-domestic-worker-bill-of-rights-veto.

6. Shah and Seville, "Domestic Worker Organizing," 431.

7. Ibid.

8. Andrea Cristina Mercado and Ai-jen Poo, "Domestic Workers Organizing in the United States," Association for Women's Rights in Development, 2008.

9. Ibid.

10. Ibid.

11. Ibid., 434.

12. Maria Distancia, telephone interview by author, San Francisco, CA, May 30, 2013.

13. Mercado and Poo, "Domestic Workers Organizing in the United States.

14. Ibid.

15. Ibid.

16. Ibid.

17. Shah and Seville, "Domestic Worker Organizing," 435.

18. California Senate Rules Committee, Bill Analysis, Assemb. B. 2536, 2005–2006 Leg., Reg. Sess. (Cal. 2006), http://www.leginfo.ca.gov/pub/05-06/bill/asm/ab_2501-2550/ab_2536_cfa_20060811_171007_sen_floor.html.

19. Assemb. B. 2536, 2005–2006 Leg., Reg. Sess. (Cal. 2006) (Governor Schwarzenegger's veto message), available at http://www.leginfo.ca.gov/pub/05-06/bill/asm/ab_2501-2550/ab_2536_vt_20060930.html.

20. Satyam Khanna, "Conservative Politicians Misleadingly Blame Labor Unions for Detroit's Woes," *ThinkProgress*, November 17, 2008, http://thinkprogress.org/politics/2008/11/17/32446/unions-auto-bailout.

21. Kate Bronfenbrenner and Dorian T. Warren, "Race, Gender, and the Rebirth of Trade Unionism," *New Labor Forum* 16, no. 3 (2007): 142–48.

22. María Fernández, "Working for Recognition," La Colectiva, 2012, http://www.lacolectivasf.org/gallery/story07.html.

23. Araceli Iñiguez, "Working for Change," La Colectiva, 2012, http://www.lacolectivasf.org/gallery/story02.html.

24. Elissa Strauss, "The Invisible Workers," *American Prospect*, May 22, 2009, http://prospect.org/article/invisible-workers.

25. Shah and Seville, "Domestic Worker Organizing," 461.

26. Ibid., 438.

27. Ibid.

28. Ibid., 461.

29. *Hearing on Assemb. B. 889 Before the Assemb. Labor Comm.*, 2011 Leg., Reg. Sess. (May 2011) (testimony of Boots Chavez).

30. Legislative Counsel's Digest, AB 889, introduced February 17, 2011,

http://www.leginfo.ca.gov/pub/11-12/bill/asm/ab_0851-0900/ab_889_bill_20110217_introduced.html.

31. California Legislative Information, AB 889 Assembly Bill, Bill Analyses, http://www.leginfo.ca.gov/pub/11-12/bill/asm/ab_0851-0900/ab_889_cfa_20120828_102413_sen_floor.html.

32. California Chamber of Commerce, "Floor Alert: AB 889 (Ammiano) Domestic Work Employees: Oppose," August 27, 2012, http://www.calchamber.com/governmentrelations/documents/ab889_senate-floor_082712.pdf.

33. Ibid.

34. Ibid.

35. Madeleine Thomas, "Proposed Domestic Workers Bill of Rights Elicits Varied Opinions," *Oakland North*, September 25, 2012, https://oaklandnorth.net/2012/09/25/proposed-domestic-workers-bill-of-rights-elicits-varied-opinions/.

36. Ibid.

37. Richard Winsten, telephone interview by author, San Francisco, CA, February 25, 2013.

38. California Association for Health Services at Home, "CAHSAH Legislative Priorities 2012," http://www.cahsah.org/documents/1212_s_2012_legislative_priorities.pdf.

39. Edmund G. Brown Jr., AB 889 veto message, September 30, 2012, http://gov.ca.gov/docs/AB_889_Veto_Message.pdf.

40. Deborah Doctor, "AB 889—Oppose Unless Amended," Disability Rights California, August 8, 2011, http://www.disabilityrightsca.org/legislature/Legislation/2011/2011-08-22%20AB%20889_Oppose-Amend%20.htm.

41. Deborah Doctor, telephone interview by author, San Francisco, CA, March 12, 2013.

42. Craig Becker. Telephone Interview by author. San Francisco, CA, May 7, 2013

43. Tom Ammiano, email interview by author, San Francisco, CA, November 27, 2012.

44. "Bill Demanding Water, Shade for Farm Workers Killed by Governor," *Sacramento Bee*, September 30, 2012, http://blogs.sacbee.com/capitolalertlatest/2012/09/a-matter----ab-2676-farmworker-heat-bill-1.html.

45. "Brown Rejects Bill to Establish Replacement Program for ADHC," Disability Rights California, July 26, 2011, http://www.disabilityrightsca.org/news/2011_newsaboutus/2011-07-26-cahealthline.html.

46. Deborah Doctor, telephone interview by author. San Francisco, CA, March 12, 2013.

47. Danielle Feris, telephone interview by author, Oakland, CA, January 25, 2013.

48. Andrea Cristina Mercado, email interview by author, San Francisco, CA, February 23, 2014.

49. Luna Ranjit, telephone interview by author, San Francisco, CA, December 30, 2012.

50. National Domestic Workers Alliance et al., *Home Truths*.

51. Mercy Albaran, telephone interview by author, San Francisco, CA, June 26, 2013.

52. Ibid.

53. Rose Arrieta, "California Domestic Workers Win Long-Sought Bill of Rights," *In These Times*, September 26, 2013, https://inthesetimes.com/working/entry/15669/california_passes_domestic_workers_bill_of_rights.

54. Deborah Doctor, "AB 241—Oppose Unless Amended," Disability Rights California, August 5, 2013, http://www.disabilityrightsca.org/legislature/Legislation/2013/materials/AB%20241%20support%20 8.6.2013.pdf.

55. Nikki Brown-Booker, telephone interview by author, San Francisco, CA, July 6, 2013.

56. Sheila Bapat, "Domestic Workers, Overtime Pay, and the Perceived 'Cost Problem,'" *RH Reality Check*, September 30, 2013, http://rhrealitycheck.org/article/2013/09/30/domestic-workers-overtime-pay-and-the-perceived-cost-problem/.

5."Domestic Insurgents"

1. Burns, "Domestic Insurgents."

2. Natalicia Tracy, telephone interview by author, San Francisco, CA, December 27, 2012.

3. Ibid.

4. Brian Lockhart, "Advocates seek domestic workers' bill," CTPost.com, March 14, 2014, http://www.ctpost.com/local/article/Advocates-seek-domestic-workers-bill-5316200.php#photo-6016810.

5. Lydia Edwards, telephone interview by author, San Francisco, CA, March 11, 2014.

6. Michael Moran, telephone interview by author, San Francisco, CA, March 12, 2014.

7. Monique Nguyen, telephone interview by author, San Francisco, CA, December 27, 2012.
8. Massachusetts Domestic Workers' Bill of Rights Fact Sheet, March 2014.
9. *Act Establishing the Domestic Workers' Bill of Rights*, H. 3884, S. 882, https://malegislature.gov/Bills/188/Senate/S882.
10. Natalicia Tracy, interview.
11. Ibid.
12. John Bishow and Donald O. Parsons, *Trends in Severance Pay Coverage in the United States: 1980–2001*, Bureau of Labor Statistics (May 2004), http://papers.ssrn.com/sol3/papers.cfm?abstract_id=878144.
13. *Act Establishing the Domestic Workers' Bill of Rights*.
14. Massachusetts Domestic Workers' Bill of Rights Fact Sheet.
15. Sheila Bapat, "Improving How Domestic Workers and Their Employers Settle Disputes," *RH Reality Check*, May 16, 2013, http://rhrealitycheck.org/article/2013/05/16/improving-how-domestic-workers-and-their-employers-settle-disputes/.
16. Lydia Edwards, telephone interview by author, San Francisco, CA, January 11, 2013.
17. Lydia Edwards, interview, March 11, 2014.
18. Bapat, "Improving How Domestic Workers and Their Employers Settle Disputes."
19. Ibid.
20. Ibid.
21. Burnham and Theodore, "Home Economics," vii.
22. Bapat, "Improving How Domestic Workers and Their Employers Settle Disputes."
23. Ibid.
24. Sona Soares, interview by author, San Francisco, CA, May 3, 2013.
25. *Domestic Workers' Bill of Rights*, SB 535, http://www.capitol.hawaii.gov/session2013/Bills/SB535_.HTM
26. Ibid.
27. Ibid.
28. *Domestic Workers' Bill of Rights*, HB 1681, http://www.capitol.hawaii.gov/Archives/measure_indiv_Archives.aspx?billtype=HB&billnumber=1681&year=2012.
29. Della Au Belatti, interview by author, San Francisco, CA, May 2, 2013.
30. Karl Rhoads, "S.B. 535, Oppose Unless Amended," North American Religious Liberty Association–West, April 29, 2013.
31. Rep. Roy Takumi, telephone interview by author, San Francisco, CA, May 2, 2013.

32. Yuxing Zheng, "Oregon House Narrowly Approves Workplace Protections for Domestic Workers," Oregonian, May 7, 2013, http://www.oregonlive.com/politics/index.ssf/2013/05/oregon_house_approves_workplac.html.

33. Sara Gelser, telephone interview by author, San Francisco, CA, July 3, 2013.

34. Ibid.

35. "Oregon to Allow Undocumented College Students to Pay the Same Tuition as Residents," Fox News Latino, April 3, 2013, http://latino.foxnews.com/latino/politics/2013/04/02/oregon-to-allow-undocumented-college-students-to-pay-same-rate-as-residents/.

36. Yuxing Zheng, "Undocumented Residents Could Obtain 4-Year Drivers' Licenses under Oregon Senate Bill," Oregonian, April 2, 2013, http://www.oregonlive.com/politics/index.ssf/2013/04/undocumented_residents_could_o.html.

37. Arise Chicago, "About Us: Faith, Labor, Action," http://arisechicago.org/about-us/.

38. Anna Jakubek, interview by author, Washington, DC, February 14, 2013.

39. Ibid.

40. Domestic Worker Bill of Rights, 98th General Assembly, State of Illinois, SB 1708, http://openstates.org/il/bills/98th/SB1708/documents/ILD00125909/.

41. Ibid.

42. Anna Jakubek, interview by author, San Francisco, CA, March 14, 2014.

43. "Black Women Advance Labor's Cause in an Unlikely Setting," American Postal Workers Union.

44. Tamieka Atkins, telephone interview by author, San Francisco, CA, March 14, 2014.

45. Tamieka Atkins, telephone interview by author, San Francisco, CA, March 21, 2013.

46. Dave Flessner, "Obamacare to Help, but Not Poorest in States Who Reject Medicaid Expansion: Tennessee, Georgia," Times Free Press, September 15, 2013, http://www.timesfreepress.com/news/2013/sep/15/tennessee-georgia-poor-left-behindobamacare-to/.

47. "National Domestic Workers Alliance Wins the 2013 Patiño Moore Legacy Award," Hispanics in Philanthropy, November 20, 2013, http://www.hiponline.org/resources/hip-blog/blog/539-national-domestic-workers-alliance-wins-the-2013-patino-moore-legacy-award.

48. Lydia Edwards, interview, March 11, 2014.

6. The Global Movement

1. Elizabeth Tang, interview by author, San Francisco, CA, April 5, 2013.
2. "Creuza Oliveira, a Domestic Worker in Brazil," United Nations Real Life Stories, http://www.un.org/en/letsfightracism/oliveira.shtml.
3. Uthara Ganesh, "Domestic Work in India," *Searchlight South Asia*, March 20, 2013, http://urbanpoverty.intellecap.com/?p=751.
4. Tania Branigan, "Foreign Domestic Workers across Asia Rise Up over Exploitation," *Guardian*, February 28, 2014, http://www.theguardian.com/world/2014/feb/28/foreign-domestic-workers-asia-exploitation.
5. Elizabeth Tang, interview by author, San Francisco, CA, April 5, 2013.
6. International Labour Organization, "Domestic Workers across the World."
7. International Labour Organization, "Domestic Work," http://www.ilo.org/ipec/areas/Childdomesticlabour/lang--en/index.htm.
8. International Labour Organization, "Domestic Workers across the World."
9. Ibid.
10. Gender across Borders, "Globalization and the Commodification of Female Domestic Work."
11. Ibid.
12. "Indonesian Maid Tortured in Saudi Arabia, Another Beaten to Death," Migrant Rights, November 19, 2010, http://www.migrant-rights.org/2010/11/19/indonesian-maid-tortured-in-saudi-arabia-another-beaten-to-death/.
13. "Maids in the Middle East: Little Better Than Slavery," *Economist*, September 2, 2010, http://www.economist.com/node/16953469
14. Gender across Borders, "Globalization and the Commodification of Female Domestic Work."
15. Ibid.
16. Simba Russeau, "The New Slavery: The Plight of Lebanon's Domestic Workers," http://www.simbarusseau.com/domestic-workers-lebanon/.
17. Gender across Borders, "Globalization and the Commodification of Female Domestic Work."
18. Ibid.
19. Ibid.
20. Ibid.
21. Ibid.
22. Margaret L. Satterthwaite, "Crossing Borders, Claiming Rights: Using Human Rights Law to Empower Women Migrant Workers," *Yale Hu-*

man Rights and Development Law Journal 8 (2005).
23. Ibid.
24. Ibid.
25. International Labour Organization, *Preventing Discrimination, Exploitation and Abuse of Women Migrant Workers: An Information Guide; Booklet 1: Why the Focus on Women International Migrant Workers* (International Labour Office, Geneva, 2003).
26. Satterthwaite, "Crossing Borders, Claiming Rights."
27. Ibid.
28. Human Rights Watch, *The ILO Domestic Workers Convention: New Standards to Fight Discrimination, Exploitation, and Abuse, 2013*, http://www.hrw.org/sites/default/files/related_material/2013ilo_dw_convention_brochure.pdf.
29. Satterthwaite, "Crossing Borders, Claiming Rights."
30. International Labour Organization, "Domestic Workers across the World."
31. Ibid.
32. Emily Rauhala, "Why Domestic Work Is a Global Issue," *Time*, March 1, 2011, http://world.time.com/2011/03/01/why-domestic-work-is-a-global-issue/.
33. Ibid.
34. Juana Flores, interview by author, Fruitvale, CA, July 11, 2013.
35. Shah and Seville, "Domestic Worker Organizing," 445.
36. Ibid.
37. IDWF, "Affiliates Names and Members," January 20, 2013. IDWF includes affiliates in the following countries: South Africa, Uganda, Benin, Mozambique, Zimbabwe, Tanzania, Kenya, Guinea, Togo, Zambia, Ghana, Burkina Faso, Malawi, Netherlands, Belgium, Switzerland, Indonesia, Nepal, Hong Kong, Sri Lanka, South Korea, Cambodia, India, United States, Peru, Jamaica, and Trinidad and Tobago.
38. Elizabeth Tang, interview by author.
39. Ibid.
40. Ibid.
41. Shah and Seville, "Domestic Worker Organizing," 445.
42. International Labour Organization, "Questions and Answers on the Convention Concerning Decent Work for Domestic Workers," June 21, 2011, http://www.ilo.org/rome/risorse-informative/per-la-stampa/articles/WCMS_158371/lang--en/index.htm
43. Elizabeth Tang, interview.
44. Keith Wright, "ILO Letter to Obama," August 19, 2011.

45. Lisa Baldez, "U.S. Drops the Ball on Women's Rights," *CNN Opinion*, March 8, 2013, http://www.cnn.com/2013/03/08/opinion/baldez-womens-equality-treaty.

46. National Domestic Workers Alliance and AFL-CIO, *Partnership Agreement Between the American Federation of Labor Congress of Industrial Organizations (AFL-CIO) and the National Domestic Workers Alliance (NDWA)*, May 10, 2011, http://en.domesticworkerrights.org/sites/default/files/NDWA_AFLCIO_Partnership_Agreement.pdf.

47. Elizabeth Tang, interview.

48. Shah and Seville, "Domestic Worker Organizing," 445.

49. "Caribbean Domestic Workers Demand Better Protections," July 7, 2013, CaribNewsDesk, http://www.caribnewsdesk.com/news/6183-caribbean-domestic-workers-demand-better-conditions.

50. Branigan, "Foreign Domestic Workers across Asia Rise Up over Exploitation."

51. International Labor Organization, "Landmark Treaty for Domestic Workers Comes into Force," September 5, 2013, http://www.ilo.org/global/standards/information-resources-and-publications/news/WCMS_220793/lang--en/index.htm.

52. International Labor Organization, "Bolivia Ratifies the Domestic Workers Convention," April 18, 2013, http://www.ilo.org/global/standards/information-resources-and-publications/news/WCMS_210941/lang--en/index.htm.

53. International Domestic Workers Federation, "A New Constitutional Amendment Takes Effect in Brazil," April 2, 2013, http://www.idwn.info/news.php?id=230.

54. International Domestic Workers Federation, "Nicaragua Ratifies C189," October 19, 2012, http://www.idwn.info/news.php?id=156&region=6.

55. International Domestic Workers Federation, http://www.IDWF.info/tags/c189.

56. International Labor Organization, "Landmark treaty for domestic workers comes into force."

57. International Domestic Workers Federation, "Indonesia: A Promise to Domestic workers, after 10 Years," March 18, 2014, http://idwfed.org/news.php?id=422.

58. "Pressure Grows to Protect Domestic Workers," Human Rights Watch, October 25, 2013, http://www.hrw.org/news/2013/10/27/pressure-grows-protect-domestic-workers.

59. Branigan, "Foreign Domestic Workers across Asia Rise Up over Exploitation."

60. International Domestic Workers Federation, "Thai Ministerial Regulations to Protect Domestic Workers' Rights Approved," November 8, 2012, http://www.idwn.info/news.php?id=167.

61. International Domestic Workers Federation, "Domestic Workers Law Passed in the Philippines," February 26, 2013, http://www.idwn.info/resource.php?id=68.

62. International Labour Organization, "Domestic Workers Across the World."

63. Ibid.

64. Ibid.

65. "Domestic Workers to Get Health Insurance," *Times of India*, June 7, 2013, http://timesofindia.indiatimes.com/city/gurgaon/Domestic-workers-to-get-health-insurance/articleshow/20469421.cms.

66. Surendra P. Gangan, "Now Maharashtran Domestic Workers to Get Benefits of Minimum Wages Act," Hindustan Times, August 29, 2013, http://www.hindustantimes.com/India-news/Mumbai/Now-Maharashtra-domestic-workers-to-get-benefits-of-minimum-wages-act/Article1-1114437.aspx.

67. International Domestic Workers Federation, "Argentina: New Act Puts Domestic Workers' Rights on the Same Level," March 19, 2013, http://www.idwn.info/news.php?id=229.

68. Mehdi al Lawati, "Indonesia Raises Minimum Wage for Domestic Workers," *Oman Observer*, March 2, 2014, http://main.omanobserver.om/?p=61083.

69. International Domestic Workers Federation, "Domestic Workers Now Have Their Own Union—Jamaica Household Workers Association," March 18, 2013, http://www.idwn.info/news.php?region=5&page=2.

70. "UAE Considering Standardised Contract for Domestic Workers," *National*, March 1, 2014, http://www.thenational.ae/uae/government/uae-considering-standardised-contract-for-domestic-workers.

71. "New Minimum Wage for Domestic Workers," *Times Live*, November 22, 2013, http://www.timeslive.co.za/local/2013/11/22/new-minimum-wage-for-domestic-workers.

72. Sharanjit Leyl, "Singapore Domestic Workers' Day Off," BBC, September 25, 2013, http://www.bbc.com/news/world-asia-24216611.

73. Samir Naji al Hasan Moqbel, "Gitmo Is Killing Me," *New York Times*, April 14, 2013, http://www.nytimes.com/2013/04/15/opinion/hunger-striking-at-guantanamo-bay.html?_r=0.

7. Collective Bargaining and Beyond

1. Melissa Gira Grant, Twitter post, June 9, 2013, https://twitter.com/melissagira.

2. Cynthia Hess, "Women and the Care Crisis: Valuing In-Home Care in Policy and Practice," Institute for Women's Policy Research, April 2013, http://www.iwpr.org/publications/pubs/women-and-the-care-crisis-valuing-in-home-care-in-policy-and-practice.

3. Stu Schneider, "Victories for Home Health Care Workers," Paraprofessional Health Care Institute, September/October 2003, http://phinational.org/sites/phinational.org/files/clearinghouse/homehealthcare.pdf.

4. Ibid.

5. "What Would/Does a Feminist Labor Movement Look Like?" *Dissent,* June 13, 2013, http://www.dissentmagazine.org/blog/audio-whatwoulddoes-a-feminist-labor-movement-look-like.

6. Michael Grabell, "The Expendables: How the Temps Who Power Corporate Giants Are Getting Crushed," *ProPublica,* June 27, 2013, http://www.propublica.org/article/the-expendables-how-the-temps-who-power-corporate-giants-are-getting-crushe.

7. Bureau of Labor Statistics, "Union Members Summary 2012," January 23, 2013, http://www.bls.gov/news.release/union2.nr0.htm.

8. Katherine Gallagher Robbins, "Women Account for 72 Percent of the Decline in Union Membership from 2011 to 2012," National Women's Law Center, January 23, 2013, http://www.nwlc.org/our-blog/women-account-72-percent-decline-union-membership-2011-2012.

9. Bureau of Labor Statistics, "Union Membership Data from the National Directory Series," ftp://ftp.bls.gov/pub/special.requests/collbarg/unmem.txt.

10. Andy Sher, "Union Hits Tennessee Gov. Bill Haslam's Plan to Abolish Teacher Pay Schedules," *Times Free Press,* January 12, 2012, http://www.timesfreepress.com/news/2012/jan/12/union-hits-haslam-plan-to-abolish-teacher-pay/.

11. Ballotpedia, "Ohio Collective Bargaining Limit Repeal 2011," http://ballotpedia.org/wiki/index.php/Ohio_Senate_Bill_5_Veto_Referendum,_Issue_2_%282011%29.

12. United Auto Workers, "Battlegrounds: Michigan Child Care Providers Stripped of Collective Bargaining Rights," March 4, 2011, http://uaw.org/articles/battlegrounds-michigan-child-care-providers-stripped-collective-bargaining-rights.

13. Sheila Bapat, "Trends in Union Membership Indicate Weak Job Pros-

pects for Women," *RH Reality Check*, January 30, 2013, http://rhrealitycheck.org/article/2013/01/30/union-membership-trends-indicate-weak-job-prospects-women-0/.

14. Ibid.
15. Bapat, "Living on the Edge of a Permanent Fiscal Cliff."
16. Brenda Carter, interview by author, January 25, 2013, San Francisco, CA.
17. Eileen Boris and Jennifer Klein, "Frontline Caregivers: Still Struggling," *Dissent*, Summer 2013, http://www.dissentmagazine.org/article/frontline-caregivers-still-struggling.
18. Schneider, "Victories for Home Health Care Workers."
19. Steven Greenhouse, "In Biggest Drive Since 1937, Union Gains a Victory," *New York Times*, February 26, 1999, http://www.nytimes.com/1999/02/26/us/in-biggest-drive-since-1937-union-gains-a-victory.html.
20. Candace Howes, "Living Wages and Retention of Homecare Workers in San Francisco," *Industrial Relations* 44 no. 1 (2005): 139–63.
21. Ibid.
22. Ibid.
23. Schneider, "Victories for Home Health Care Workers."
24. Matt Mayers, interview by author, San Francisco, CA, May 17, 2013.
25. Clyde Weiss, "Vermont Home Care Providers Win Historic Collective Bargaining Victory," AFSCME, May 2, 2013, http://www.afscme.org/blog/vermont-home-care-providers-win-historic-collective-bargaining-victory.
26. Janelle Blake, interview by author, San Francisco, CA, May 15, 2013.
27. Ibid.
28. Boris and Klein, "Frontline Caregivers: Still Struggling."
29. Sarah Jaffe, "A Day without Care," *Jacobin* 10 (April–May 2013), https://www.jacobinmag.com/2013/04/a-day-without-care/.
30. *Pamela Harris, et al., Petitioners v. Pat Quinn, Governor of Illinois, et al.*, Supreme Court oral argument, January 21, 2014, http://www.supremecourt.gov/oral_arguments/argument_transcripts/11-681_8mj8.pdf.
31. *Harris v. Quinn*, 656 F. 3d 692 (7th Cir. 2011), citing *Railway Employees Dept. v. Hanson* 351 U.S. 225 (1956) and *Abood v. Detroit Board of Ed.*, 431 U.S. 209 (1977).
32. "Brief for Amici Curiae Homecare Historians in Support of Respondents," December 2013, http://www.americanbar.org/content/dam/aba/publications/supreme_court_preview/briefs-v3/11-681_resp_amcu_hh.authcheckdam.pdf.

33. Ibid.
34. Laura Reyes, "The Sexist Agenda Hidden in *Harris v. Quinn*," *Huffington Post*, February 12, 2014, http://www.huffingtonpost.com/laurareyes/the-sexist-agenda-income-inequality_b_4770059.html.
35. Domestic Workers United, National Domestic Workers Alliance, and Urban Justice Center, *Domestic Workers and Collective Bargaining*.
36. New York State Department of Labor, *Feasibility of Domestic Worker Organizing*, November 2, 2010, http://www.labor.ny.gov/legal/laws/pdf/domestic-workers/domestic-workers-feasibility-study.pdf.
37. Ibid.
38. Domestic Workers United et al., *Domestic Workers and Collective Bargaining*.
39. Burns, "Domestic Insurgents."
40. Josh Eidelson, "Alt-Labor," *American Prospect*, January 29, 2013, http://prospect.org/article/alt-labor.
41. Josh Eidelson, "Guest Workers as Bellwether," *Dissent*, Spring 2013, http://www.dissentmagazine.org/article/guest-workers-as-bellwether.
42. "The Third Shift: Child Care Needs and Access for Working Mothers in Restaurants," ROC United, July 1, 2013, http://rocunited.org/the-third-shift/.
43. Eidelson, "Alt-Labor."
44. Saru Jayaraman, interview by author, Oakland, CA, February 23, 2013.
45. Alex Tom, interview by author, San Francisco, CA, June 14, 2013.
46. "Workers Organizing Center," Chinese Progressive Association, http://www.cpasf.org/workeroganizingcenter.
47. Laura Safer Espinoza, interview by author, San Francisco, CA, July 5, 2013.
48. Bernice Yeung and Grace Rubenstein, "Female Workers Face Rape, Harassment in U.S. Agriculture Industry," *Frontline*, June 25, 2013, http://www.pbs.org/wgbh/pages/frontline/social-issues/rape-in-the-fields/female-workers-face-rape-harassment-in-u-s-agriculture-industry/.
49. Mónica Ramírez, "Farmworker Women Leaders Making Major Impact," *Latino Rebels*, March 26, 2014, http://www.latinorebels.com/2014/03/26/farmworker-women-leaders-making-major-impact/.
50. Paul Saginaw, co-founder of Zingerman's, interview by author, San Francisco, CA, February 24, 2013.
51. Ibid.
52. Rocio Avila, interview by author, San Francisco, CA, February 1, 2013.
53. Jess Kutch, interview by author, San Francisco, CA, April 10, 2013.
54. Kutch, interview.

55. A representative from Juicy Couture said via email on April 15, 2013, that the company has "no such policy with regard to employee hours nor have any decisions been made about how to best manage ACA requirements" and that the company is "still reviewing the ACA's impact and how to best continue to provide meaningful benefits options to our managers and associates."

56. Steven Greenhouse, "A Part-Time Life, as Hours Shrink and Shift," *New York Times*, October 27, 2012, http://www.nytimes.com/2012/10/28/business/a-part-time-life-as-hours-shrink-and-shift-for-american-workers.html?pagewanted=all&_r=0.

57. Ibid.

58. Jenna Sauers, "Juicy Couture Is Cutting Worker Hours to Avoid Paying for Employee Health Care," *Jezebel*, April 1, 2013, http://jezebel.com/5993179/juicy-couture-is-cutting-worker-hours-to-avoid-paying-for-employee-health-care.

59. Retail Action Project, "New Study Shows Gender Gap in Pay, Benefits, and Promotions for Women in Retail," December 21, 2011, http://retailactionproject.org/2011/12/new-study-shows-gender-gap-in-pay-benefits-promotions-for-women-in-retail/.

60. Sheila Bapat, "Workers Organize to Fight the Part Timeification Trend at Juicy Couture, Other Chains," *RH Reality Check*, April 21, 2013, http://rhrealitycheck.org/article/2013/04/21/workers-organize-to-fight-the-part-timeification-trend-at-juicy-couture-other-chains/.

61. Ali, interview by author, San Francisco, CA, April 9, 2013.

62. Email from Juicy Couture representative, April 15, 2013.

63. Sara Ziff, interview by author, Washington, DC, February 18, 2013.

64. Ibid.

65. Drew Grant, "The Sorrow and the Pretty: Model Alliance Looks to Empower the Ridiculously Good-Looking," *New York Observer*, September 4, 2012, http://observer.com/2012/09/the-sorrow-and-the-pretty-model-alliance-looks-to-empower-the-really-really-ridiculously-good-looking/.

66. Jenna Sauers, "Mark Jacobs Doesn't Pay His Models, Says Model," *Jezebel*, March 5, 2012, http://jezebel.com/5889757/marc-jacobs-doesnt-pay-his-models-said-model.

67. Ashley Mears, "Why Modeling Is, Technically Speaking, a Bad Job," Model Alliance, http://modelalliance.org/2012/1621/1621.

68. Independent Democratic Conference, *New York's Modeling Crisis: The Importance of Providing Legal Protections for Child Models*, June 2013, http://librables.com/p/11329848.

69. Ibid.

70. Anna Durrett, interview by author, San Francisco, CA, June 25, 2013.

71. Sara Ziff, "Regardless of Age, It's About Rights," *New York Times*, November 12, 2012, http://www.nytimes.com/roomfordebate/2012/09/13/sweet-16-and-a-runway-model/regardless-of-a-fashion-models-age-its-about-rights.

72. Nora Crotty, "New York Signs Law Protecting Child Models' Labor Rights," *Fashionista*, October 22, 2013, http://fashionista.com/2013/10/new-york-signs-law-protecting-child-models-labor-rights/.

73. Amy Odell, "New York Passes Child Model Law," *BuzzFeed*, June 12, 2013, http://www.buzzfeed.com/amyodell/new-york-passes-child-model-law.

74. Marion G. Crain, "An Imminent Hanging," *ABA Journal of Labor and Employment Law* 26 (2011): 151; Washington University in St. Louis Legal Studies Research Paper No. 10-08-02.

75. *Vance v. Ball State*, 133 S.C. 2434 (2013).

8. Valuing Care Means Valuing Parents

1. Nancy Folbre, ed., *For Love and Money: Care Provision in the United States* (New York: Russel Sage Foundation, 2012): 110.

2. "Selected Long-Term Care Statistics," Family Caregiver Alliance, http://caregiver.org/selected-long-term-care-statistics.

3. "Projected Future Growth of the Older Population." Department of Health and Human Services, Administration on Aging. http://www.aoa.gov/Aging_Statistics/future_growth/future_growth.aspx#age

4. T. Alan Lacy and Benjamin Wright, "Occupational Employment Projections to 2018," Bureau of Labor Statistics, December 22, 2010, http://www.bls.gov/opub/mlr/2009/11/art5full.pdf.

5. Folbre, *For Love and Money*.

6. "Our Policy Pillars," Caring across Generations, http://www.caringacross.org/about-us/.

7. Sarita Gupta, interview by author, Washington, DC, February 15, 2013.

8. Sharon Lerner, "Will the Latest Push for Paid Family Leave in New York Succeed?" Demos.org, March 6, 2014, http://www.demos.org/blog/3/6/14/will-latest-push-paid-family-leave-new-york-succeed.

9. Kate Taylor, "New York City Council Swiftly Passes Bill to Extend Paid Sick Days," *New York Times*, February 26, 2014, http://www.nytimes.com/2014/02/27/nyregion/new-york-city-council-swiftly-passes-bill-to-extend-paid-sick-days.html?_r=2.

10. Bryce Covert, "The Secret Benefits of Paid Sick Days for All," *ThinkProgress*, March 13, 2014, http://thinkprogress.org/economy/2014/03/13/3400731/paid-sick-days-benefits/.

11. Debra L. Ness, "Vote to Strengthen New York City's Sick Days Law Shows Lawmakers Are in Touch with Working Families," National Partnership for Women and Families, February 26, 2014, http://www.nationalpartnership.org/news-room/press-releases/vote-to-strengthen-new-york-citys-sick-days-law-shows-lawmakers-are-in-touch-with-working-families.html.

12. Vicki Shabo, telephone interview by author, San Francisco, CA, June 18, 2013.

13. Democracy Corps, Greenberg Quinlan Rosner, and Women's Voices, Women Vote Action Fund, "The Women's Economic Agenda," July 22, 2013, http://www.democracycorps.com/attachments/article/948/dcor.wvwv.memo.072213.final.pdf.

14. Shabo, interview.

15. Cassandra D. Engeman, *Ten Years of the California Paid Family Leave Program: Strengthening Commitment to Work, Affirming Commitment to Family* (Santa Barbara: Center for Study of Work, Labor and Democracy, University of California: 2012), http://www.femst.ucsb.edu/projects/crwsj/engagements/pdf/Engeman-PFL-Policy-Brief.pdf.

16. Bryce Covert, "Rhode Island Poised to Be Third State with Paid Family Leave," *Think Progress*, July 3, 2013, http://thinkprogress.org/economy/2013/07/03/2251881/rhode-island-paid-family-leave-passage/.

17. "Washington House OKs Bill Indefinitely Postponing Paid Family Leave," Associated Press, June 28, 2013, http://www.oregonlive.com/politics/index.ssf/2013/06/washington_house_oks_bill_inde.html.

18. Jane M. Von Bergen, "Praise for N.J.'s Family Leave Insurance," Philly.com, May 5, 2013, http://articles.philly.com/2013-05-05/news/39028647_1_insurance-program-fmla-employers.

19. Ibid.

20. "Get Your Ass Back to Work," National Partnership for Women and Families, April 3, 2014.

21. Lauren Weber, "Why Dads Don't Take Paternity Leave," *Wall Street Journal*, June 12, 2013, http://online.wsj.com/news/articles/SB10001424127887324049504578541633708283670.

22. "Milestones in Mayer's Tenure as Yahoo's Chief," *New York Times*, January 16, 2014, http://www.nytimes.com/interactive/2014/01/16/technology/marissa-mayer-yahoo-timeline.html#/#time303_8396.

23. Shabo, interview.

24. Jia Lynn Yang, "AOL Chief Cuts 401(k) Benefits, Blames Obamacare and Two 'Distressed Babies,'" *Washington Post*, February 7, 2014, http://www.washingtonpost.com/blogs/wonkblog/wp/2014/02/06/aol-chief-cuts-401k-benefits-blames-obamacare/.

25. Derek Thompson, "AOL Is the Weirdest Successful Tech Company in America," Atlantic.com, February 8, 2013, http://www.theatlantic.com/business/archive/2013/02/aol-is-the-weirdest-successful-tech-company-in-america/272993/.

26. Edmund Lee and Michelle Yun, "AOL Chief Apologizes for 'Distressed Babies' Comment," Bloomberg.com, February 10, 2014, http://www.bloomberg.com/news/2014-02-09/aol-s-armstrong-apologizes-after-401-k-gaffe-stirs-controversy.html.

27. "2013 Working Mother 100 Best Companies: AOL," Working Mother, http://www.workingmother.com/best-companies/aol-5.

28. Engeman, *Ten Years of the California Paid Family Leave Program: Strengthening Commitment to Work, Affirming Commitment to Family.*

29. Omar Akhtar, "The 25 Best Medium-Size Companies to Work For," CNN Money, October 29, 2012, http://money.cnn.com/gallery/news/companies/2012/10/25/best-medium-companies.fortune/5.html.

30. "Costco's Profit Soars to $537 Million Just Days after CEO Endorses Minimum Wage Increase," *Huffington Post*, March 13, 2013, http://www.huffingtonpost.com/2013/03/12/costco-profit_n_2859250.html.

31. Ryan Coonerty and Jeremy Neuner, *The Rise of the Naked Economy: How to Benefit from the Changing Workplace* (New York: Palgrave McMillan, 2013): 193–94.

32. Sheila Bapat, "Businesses Must Improve Their Family Policies—for Distressed Babies and All Workers," *RH Reality Check*, March 7, 2014.,http://rhrealitycheck.org/article/2014/03/07/businesses-must-improve-family-policies-distressed-babies-workers/.

33. Karen Schulman and Helen Blank, P*ivot Point: State Childcare Assistance Policies 2013* (National Women's Law Center, 2013), http://www.nwlc.org/sites/default/files/pdfs/final_nwlc_2013statechildcareassistancereport.pdf.

34. Schulman and Blank, *State Childcare Assistance Policies 2011* (National Women's Law Center, 2011), http://www.nwlc.org/sites/default/files/pdfs/state_child_care_assistance_policies_report2011_final.pdf.

35. Schulman and Blank, *Downward Slide: State Childcare Assistance Policies 2012* (National Women's Law Center, 2012), http://www.nwlc.org/resource/downward-slide-state-child-care-assistance-policies-2012.

36. Schulman and Blank, Pivot Point.

37. Ibid.

38. Tim Worstall, "Why We Can't End Poverty in America: It's the Ignorance," *Forbes*, July 29, 2012, http://www.forbes.com/sites/timworstall/2012/07/29/why-we-cant-end-poverty-in-america-its-the-ignorance/.

39. Sheila Bapat, "Childcare Increasingly Expensive, Even as Public Assistance for Low-Income Families Declines," *RH Reality Check*, October 25, 2012, http://rhrealitycheck.org/article/2012/10/25/child-care-is-increasingly-expensive-but-public-funding-decreasing-since-2001/.

40. Ibid.

41. Schulman and Blank, *Downward Slide.*

42. Ibid.

43. Bapat, "Childcare Increasingly Expensive."

44. Jaffe, "A Day without Care."

45. David Levitus, interview by author, San Francisco, CA, May 9, 2013.

46. Ibid.

47. Amy Dean, "Old Roots, New Branches: Jewish Spiritual Communities and the Rise of Alt-Labor," *Tikkun*, July 3, 2013, http://www.tikkun.org/nextgen/old-roots-new-branches-jewish-spiritual-communities-and-the-rise-of-alt-labor.

48. Meg Yardley, interview by author, San Francisco, CA, July 7, 2013.

49. Sheila Bapat, "Portrayal of Domestic Workers in Popular Culture," *Bitch* 63 (Summer 2014; forthcoming).

50. "Cast Your Vote for the National Domestic Workers Alliance," NDWA, November 2, 2012.

51. "Amy Poehler: Support the CA Domestic Workers Bill of Rights," YouTube video, 1:00, posted by "domestic workers," August 23, 2012, https://www.youtube.com/watch?v=pH3QsIafKHs&noredirect=1.

52. "Get Your Ass Back to Work," National Partnership for Women and Families.

9. Immigration Reform

1. AJ Vicens, "The Obama Administration's 2 Million Deportations, Explained," *Mother Jones*, April 4, 2014, http://www.motherjones.com/politics/2014/04/obama-administration-record-deportations.

2. Chris Hayes, "President Obama: Stop Waiting on Deportations," MSNBC, April 11, 2014, http://www.msnbc.com/all-in/watch/President-obama-stop-waiting-on-deportations-223944771734.

3. Burnham and Theodore, "Home Economics."

4. Cynthia Hess and Jane Henrici, "Increasing Pathways to Legal Status for Immigrant In-Home Care Workers," Institute for Women's Policy Research, February 2013, http://www.iwpr.org/publications/pubs/increasing-pathways-to-legal-status-for-immigrant-in-home-care-workers/.

5. National Guestworker Alliance, "The POWER Act Fact Sheet," http://thepoweract.com/wp-content/uploads/2010/08/POWER-Act-factsheet-revised.pdf, accessed on April 20, 2014.

6. Rebecca Smith and Eunice Hyunhye Cho, "Workers' Rights on ICE: How Immigration Reform Can Stop Retaliation and Advance Labor Rights," National Employment Law Project, February 2013, http://nelp.3cdn.net/0e04248130076eb182_6am6boifj.pdf.

7. Ibid.

8. Hollis Pfitsch, telephone interview by author, San Francisco, CA, April 15, 2013.

9. Ibid.

10. National Immigration Law Center, "How Errors in E-Verify Databases Impact U.S. Citizens and Lawfully Present Immigrants," February 2011, http://www.nilc.org/workerseverify.html.

11. U.S. Citizenship and Immigration Services, "What is E-Verify?" http://www.uscis.gov/e-verify/what-e-verify, accessed on April 20, 2014.

12. Smith and Cho, "Workers' Rights on ICE."

13. Ibid.

14. "Remarks by the President on Comprehensive Immigration Reform," White House, January 29, 2013, http://www.whitehouse.gov/the-press-office/2013/01/29/remarks-president-comprehensive-immigration-reform.

15. Ashley Parker, "House Immigration Bill Is Said to Offer 3 Paths," *New York Times*, April 2, 2013, http://www.nytimes.com/2013/04/03/us/politics/house-groups-immigration-bill-takes-shape.html?_r=1&.

16. Bryce Covert, "How to Include Domestic Workers in Immigration Reform," *Nation*, February 12, 2013, http://www.thenation.com/blog/172846/how-include-domestic-workers-immigration-reform#.

17. Jennifer Martinez, "Microsoft, Intel, Qualcomm Push for Immigration Reform Ahead of Senate Debate," Hill, June 10, 2013, http://thehill.com/blogs/hillicon-valley/technology/304541-microsoft-intel-qualcomm-push-for-immigration-reform-ahead-of-senate-debate-.

18. Nikki Brown-Booker, telephone interview by author, San Francisco, CA, July 6, 2013.

19. "We Belong Together," National Domestic Workers Alliance, http://www.domesticworkers.org/es/we-belong-together.

20. Silvia Lopez, telephone interview by author, San Francisco, CA, February 15, 2013.
21. Ibid.
22. Ibid.
23. Ai-jen Poo, in-person interview by author, New York City, October 11, 2012.
24. We Belong Together: Women for Common-Sense Immigration Reform, "Analysis of Senate Immigration Bill Amendments: Impact on Women and Families," Accessed April 20, 2014.http://www.webelongtogether.org/sites/default/files/ENG_Amendments_Results.pdf.
25. Ibid.
26. Ibid.
27. Ibid.
28. Ai-jen Poo, "Making Immigration Reform Work for Working Women," March 18, 2013, (testimony submitted to US Senate Committee on the Judiciary), http://www.domesticworkers.org/news/2013/making-immigration-reform-work-for-working-women.
29. Ibid.
30. "Workplace Violations, Immigration Status, and Gender: Summary of Findings from the 2008 Unregulated Work Survey," National Employment Law Project, August 2011, http://www.nelp.org/page/-/Justice/2011/Fact_Sheet_Workplace_Violations_Immigration_Gender.pdf?nocdn=1.
31. Poo, "Making Immigration Reform Work for Working Women."
32. We Belong Together, "Analysis of Senate Immigration Bill Amendments."
33. Ai-jen Poo, "A Big Step Forward," email from National Domestic Workers Alliance, June 28, 2013.
34. Verónica Bayetti Flores, "Immigration Reform Bill Clears Senate, but Is It a Feminist Win?" Feministing, June 28, 2013, http://feministing.com/2013/06/28/immigration-reform-bill-clears-senate-but-is-it-a-feminist-win/.
35. "Senate Passes Hoeven-Corker Amendment with Overwhelming Support," website of John Hoeven, June 26, 2013, http://www.hoeven.senate.gov/public/index.cfm/2013/6/senate-passes-hoeven-corker-amendment-with-overwhelming-support.
36. "The Hoeven-Corker Amendment: Myth vs. Fact," website of John Hoeven, June 24, 2013, http://www.hoeven.senate.gov/public/index.cfm/2013/6/the-hoeven-corker-amendment-myth-vs-fact.
37. Jessica González-Rojas, "Fenced In and Locked Out: Border Deal

Will Endanger Women's Lives," *Huffington Post*, June 26, 2013, http://www.huffingtonpost.com/jessica-gonzalezrojas/fenced-in-and-locked-out_b_3498971.html.

38. Poo, "Making Immigration Reform Work for Working Women."

39. Ibid.

40. Hess and Henrici, "Increasing Pathways to Legal Status for Immigrant In-Home Care Workers."

41. Poo, "Making Immigration Reform Work for Working Women."

42. Ibid.

43. Ibid.

44. Ibid.

45. Hess and Henrici, "Increasing Pathways to Legal Status for Immigrant In-Home Care Workers.

46. Ai-jen Poo, "The Plight of the 'Illegal' Nanny," *Time*, March 6, 2013, http://ideas.time.com/2013/03/06/the-plight-of-the-illegal-nanny/.

47. Matt O'Brien, "High-Skilled Immigration Debate Grows over Stark Gender Imbalance, Favoring Men for H-1B Visas," Contra Costa Times, March 18, 2013, http://www.contracostatimes.com/News/ci_22819054/Highskilled-immigration-debate-grows-over-stark.

48. "We Belong Together Commends Executive Action Authorizing Employment of Spouses of H1B Visa Holders," Email alert, April 10, 2014.

49. Jonathan Weisman, "Boehner Doubts Immigration Bill Will Pass in 2014," *New York Times*, February 6, 2014, http://www.nytimes.com/2014/02/07/us/politics/boehner-doubts-immigration-overhaul-will-pass-this-year.html?_r=0.

Conclusion and Policy Recommendations

1. Douglas Martin, "Evelyn Coke, Home Care Aide Who Fought Pay Rule, Is Dead at 74," *New York Times*, August 9, 2009, http://www.nytimes.com/2009/08/10/nyregion/10coke.html.

2. Shah and Seville, "Domestic Worker Organizing," 414.

3. 29 U. S. C. §213(a)(15); 29 CFR §552.109(a).

4. Steven Greenhouse, "U.S. to Include Home Care Aides in Wage and Overtime Law," *New York Times*, September 17, 2013, http://www.nytimes.com/2013/09/18/business/us-to-include-home-care-workers-in-wage-and-overtime-law.html.

5. Martin, "Evelyn Coke, Home Care Aide Who Fought Pay Rule, Is Dead at 74."

6. Ibid.

7. "Long Island Care at Home, Ltd. v. Coke," Oyez Project at IIT Chica-

go-Kent College of Law, accessed April 5, 2014, http://www.oyez.org/cases/2000-2009/2006/2006_06_593.

8. Craig Becker, interview by author, San Francisco, CA, May 7, 2013.

9. Martin, "Evelyn Coke, Home Care Aide Who Fought Pay Rule, Is Dead at 74."

10. Ibid.

11. Ibid.

12. Michael A. Memoli, "Labor Secretary Hilda Solis Stepping Down from Office," *Los Angeles Times*, January 9, 2013, http://articles.latimes.com/2013/jan/09/news/la-pn-labor-secretary-hilda-solis-resigning-20130109.

13. "CASA de Maryland Celebrates the Appointment of Tom Perez as Secretary of Labor," CASA de Maryland, July 18, 2013, http://www.casademaryland.org/press-release/2039-casa-de-maryland-celebrates-the-appointment-of-tom-perez-as-secretary-of-labor.

14. Sheila Bapat, "Finally Domestic Workers Get Basic Labor Protections," *RH Reality Check*, September 18, 2013, http://rhrealitycheck.org/article/2013/09/18/finally-domestic-workers-get-basic-labor-protections/.

15. Greenhouse, "U.S. to Include Home Care Aides in Wage and Overtime Law."

16. Sarah Leberstein, email interview by author, San Francisco, CA, September 17, 2013.

17. "Presidential Memorandum: Updating and Modernizing Overtime Regulations," White House, March 13, 2014, http://www.whitehouse.gov/the-press-office/2014/03/13/presidential-memorandum-updating-and-modernizing-overtime-regulations.

18. Ross Eisenbrey, "Updating Overtime Rules Could Raise Wages for Millions," Economic Policy Institute, March 12, 2014, http://www.epi.org/publication/updating-overtime-rules-raise-wages-millions/.

19. "Rights Begin at Home: Protecting Yourself as a Domestic Worker," National Employment Law Project and Domestic Workers United, November 2010, http://www.nelp.org/page/-/Justice/2011/RightsBeginatHome.pdf?nocdn=1.

20. Ibid.

21. Karen Keesler, telephone interview by author, San Francisco, CA, March 25, 2013.

22. Holly J. Mitchell, "Viewpoints: California's Domestic Workers Get a Raw Deal in Budget," *Sacramento Bee*, March 13, 2014, http://www.sacbee.com/2014/03/13/6231935/viewpoints-capping-ihss-work-hours.html.

23. Nikki Brown-Booker, telephone interview by author, San Francisco, CA, July 6, 2013.

24. Josh Eidelson, "Workers Tell OSHA They Were Locked Inside Target Stores Overnight," *Nation*, January 24, 2013, http://www.thenation.com/blog/172426/workers-locked-inside-target-stores-overnight.

25. Sheila Bapat, "Did an Indian Diplomat in the United States Mistreat Her Domestic Worker?" *RH Reality Check*, January 7, 2014, http://rhrealitycheck.org/article/2014/01/07/did-an-indian-diplomat-in-the-united-states-mistreat-her-domestic-worker/.

26. Boris and Klein, "Frontline Caregivers: Still Struggling."

27. Priscilla Gonzalez, interview, April 6, 2013.